STOIC CHOICES

EPICTETUS' DISCOURES BOOK 2

STOICISM IN PLAIN ENGLISH

DR CHUCK CHAKRAPANI

THE STOIC GYM PUBLICATIONS

Stoic Gym Publications
www.thestoicgym.com

Ordering Information:
Quantity sales. Discounts are available on quantity purchases by corporations, associations, and others. For details, contact the "Special Sales Department" at the address above.

Stoic Foundations/Chuck Chakrapani. —1st ed.
ISBNs:
Print: 978-0-920219-28-7
ePub: 978-0-920219-30-0
Mobi: 978-0-920219-31-7
PDF: 978-0-920219-29-4
17 18 19 20 21 22 23 24 25 26   1 2 3 4 5 6 7 8 9 0

Contents

Stoic Choices 1

1. When to Be Confident When to Be Cautious 5

2. Choose Not to Go After External Things 13

3. Should You Seek Recommendations? 17

4. Choose to Be Faithful 19

5. Choose Only Among Things You Control 23

6. Should You Fear What You Don't Control? 29

7. Should You Fear the Future? 35

8. Choose to Look After Your Inherent Qualities 39

9. Choose to Act on Your Knowledge 45

10. Choose to Play Your Different Roles Well 51

11. Have Standards to Evaluate Your Principles 57

12. Choose the Right Way to Argue 63

13. Choose Knowledge over Anxiety 69

14. Choose to Align Your Desires with Reality 75

15. Base Your Decisions on Sound Foundation 81

16. Our Choices Give Rise to Good and Evil 85

17. Knowledge is Worthless without Practice 95

18. Choose Habits That Fight Impressions 102

19. Choose to Practice, Not to Argue Cleverly 109

20. Choose the Right Doctrine to Guide You 117

21. Guard Against Your Inconsistencies 125

22. Choose to Be a True Friend 131

23. Choice is Your Best Faculty, Don't Be Distracted 139

24. Show Yourself to Be Worthy 149

25. Why is Logic Needed? 157

26. Become Skillful in Correcting Contradictions...............159
ABOUT THE AUTHOR 162
Also by the Author..163

Stoic Choices

This is the second book of Epictetus' *Discourses*. The first book, *Stoic Foundations*, discusses the basic themes of Stoicism. Even if we fully understand them, we may not always be sure what to do when it comes to practicing the basic principles. We often face choices and the course of action in not always clear. When we meet a decision fork on the Stoic road, which path to take?

In this second book of Epictetus' *Discourses* (*Stoic Choices*), Epictetus talks about the various choices you are likely to face in real life and shows the right path to take.

Basic choices: A quick outline

Like *Stoic Foundations*, *Stoic Choices* revolves around a few themes that are also repeated in other places throughout *Discourses*. Here are some of the basic choices discussed in this book:

1. *What should you act upon: External things or internal things?* This is one of the most fundamental choices one can make. Things under your control are internal to you. Things not under your control are external to you. Therefore, if you confine your choices to what is under your control, you will be free, happy, and serene. But if you start choosing things that are not under your control you will be hindered. What is not under your control is neither good nor bad and you don't have to fear it. There is no reason to fear the future. [1, 5, 6, 7]

2. *When should you choose to be confident and when to be cautious in making decisions?* There is a basic rule for decision making: If the decision depends on your choice, be cautious. If it does not, be confident. [1]

3. *What should you protect: Your inherent qualities or qualities that are not inherent to you?* We are born with excellent qualities: Modesty, faithfulness, dignity, patience, calmness, and poise. Animals and plants don't have these qualities. You can be godlike if you cultivate and defend the qualities you were born with. [8]

4. *Is there a choice between knowledge and action?* Knowledge is important. However, a quality is preserved when it is acted upon. For example, modesty is preserved through modest actions. Anyone can talk the talk. What differentiates a Stoic practitioner is consistent action that relates to Stoic principles. [9, 19]

5. *Is there a choice between knowledge and anxiety?* Anxiety arises because you want something from others or the outside world and you think you may not get it. But the external world is not under your control and it has nothing that you need. Once you train yourself to align your desires and aversions in line with what happens, there is no need to be anxious. Your anxiety is the result of unexamined assumptions. [14, 15]

6. *Should you study logic and why?* We may agree on basic principles, but we may apply them incorrectly, unless we apply logic. If we don't know logic, we can confuse ourselves and others. Logic also helps us to choose the correct doctrine that we should follow. In fact, logic is needed even to know if logic is needed. Guard yourself against inconsistencies. [11, 12, 17, 20, 21, 25]

7. *Choose to be faithful.* We are born to be faithful. We compromise our humanity when we are not faithful. We have distinct roles to play – father, son, daughter, friend, etc. Play these roles fully and faithfully. Be a loyal friend. [3, 10, 22]

8. *Choose habits that fight false impressions.* When you repeat a behavior, it becomes a habit. Because our behavior is the result of impressions, the best way to fight false impressions is to form habits that will fight false impressions. [18]

9. *Show yourself to be worthy.* If you want a knowledgeable person talk to you, show yourself to

be worthy of his or her time. Don't seek recommendations from others. [4, 25]

10. *Choose to be skillful.* If you want to change people learn how to point out their contradictions skillfully. Be aware what is truly important and don't be distracted by faculties that are useful, but not important. [23, 26]

References

- The numbers in square brackets in this section refer to the discourse number.
- The letters after specific quotes in the book refer to the translators. They also happen to be the sources I relied on most often.
  - [WO] William A. Oldfather
  - [RD] Robert Dobbin, Penguin Classics
  - [CG/RH] Christopher Gill (ed.)/Robin Hard, Everyman
  - [RH] Robin Hard, Oxford World's Classics
  - [GL] George Long, Delphi Classics
- Any other text in square brackets is not part of the original text but inserted by me for clarification or as a commentary. I have chosen this method to avoid readers going back and forth between the text and endnotes.
- The first and last sections (*Key ideas of this discourse* and *Think about this)* are set in italics to remind readers they are not a part of the original text but are added to reinforce the ideas of the discourse.

When to Be Confident
When to Be Cautious

Key ideas of this discourse

1. We should be confident in what does not depend on our choice and be cautious in what does. But we do the opposite.

2. Death and pain are not frightening; it is the fear of death and pain that scares us.

3. All we are afraid of is nothing more than scary masks. They have no substance.

4. Only the educated – who know and practice these things – are free.

5. Be content to be thought of as a nobody if you know that you never fail to get what you want and avoid what you don't want.

Be cautious in your choices; be confident about other things

It may sound strange to some people when philosophers say that we should do everything both with confidence and caution. All the same, let's examine if we can really combine confidence with caution in everything that we do. Confidence and caution appear contradictory and not compatible with each other. How, then, can they coexist? If we are talking about confidence and caution existing in the same things, then we can rightly be accused of trying to combine the opposites.

But is it as strange as it sounds? We have often said, shown, and proved, that

1. Use of impressions represents for us the essence of good and evil; and

2. What lies outside our area of choice is not good or evil.

If these are true, what is strange about the philosopher's statement, "In things that lie outside the area of your choice, be confident; in things that lie within it, be cautious?"

As evil is a matter of exercising our choice, we need to be cautious there; as everything that is not under our control is neither good nor bad and therefore nothing to us, we can be confident regarding these things. And so, that's how we can be cautious and confident at the same time – we are confident because of our caution. Because we are cautious about evil things, we approach things that are not evil with confidence.

But we are confused and do the opposite.

We act like deer that, frightened by feathers, seek safety in hunters' nets. They meet their untimely death by confusing caution with confidence. It is so with us. We show fear in matters outside of our control but show confidence in our choice, as though there is no danger. To be deceived, to be careless or hasty, to act shamelessly, or to indulgence in uncontrolled desires – none of these matters to us if we have success in matters outside our area of choice. With respect to death, exile, pain, and ill repute, we become agitated and show a tendency to retreat.

So, as is typical of those who get the things of greatest importance wrong, we distort natural confidence into rashness, recklessness, and shamelessness. At the same time, we exchange our natural caution and self-respect for cowardice and timidity. We are full of fear and agitation. If you desire to transfer caution to your area of choice and things related to it, your desire alone will bring with it the power to avoid. If you, on the other hand, direct your desire at what is not under your control, trying to avoid what is under someone else's control, you will surely meet with fear, upset, and confusion.

We are frightened by scary masks

Death and pain are not frightening, but the fear of death and pain are. That's why we praise the person who said, "Death is no ill, but dying like a coward is."

So be confident about death but be cautious of the fear of death – the opposite of what we are doing now. We are afraid of death. Yet, when we form a judgment about it we do so with carelessness, disregard, and unconcern. Socrates aptly called our fears "scary masks." Masks appear scary and frighten children, because they haven't seen them before. We react to events similarly and for the same reason. What is a child? Ignorant and uninstructed. In so far as the child has knowledge, it is equal to us.

"What is death?"

"A scary mask. Take it off. See, it doesn't bite."

Sooner or later, body and soul will separate, as they formerly were. Why be upset if it happens now? If it is not now, it will be later. Why? To be a part of the cycle of change. The universe needs some things to come into being now and some things later. It needs things whose time is now complete.

"What is pain?"

"A scary mask. Turn it around and look."

Our flesh is affected by impressions – sometimes hard, sometimes smooth. If it is not worth your while, the door is always open; if it is, bear it. As the door always remains open, our problems disappear."

"What is the result of following these principles?"

"Exactly the best and the most beautiful, as it should be for the truly educated: tranquility, fearlessness and freedom."

[*By the phrase "The door is open" Stoics refer to taking one's own life. While they did not advocate mindless suicide, they were not against it when carried out for a rational purpose. There are a couple of discourses in which Epictetus dissuades people from committing suicide for the wrong reason.*]

Only the educated are free

It is not, as common people say, that, "Only the free can be educated." Rather it is, as philosophers say, "only the educated are free."

"How so?"

"Is freedom anything but the right to live the way we wish?"

"Nothing."

"Do you wish to live in error?"

"No"

"Then no one who lives in error is free. Do you wish to live in fear, grief, and sorrow?"

"Of course not."

"This means that no one who lives in fear, grief, or sorrow is free. But anyone who doesn't live in fear, grief, and sorrow is free. Then how can we trust legislators who say that only the freeborn are entitled to any education? Don't philosophers say that only the educated are free?"

"What about the master who performs a ceremony to free his slave? Hasn't he accomplished anything?"

"He certainly has. He has performed the ceremony and has paid five percent tax to the state."

"But hasn't the slave won his freedom?"

"No more than he has achieved peace of mind. "

You may grant freedom to others. But who your master is, I wonder. Money? Women? Boys? A tyrant? A friend of a tyrant? It must be one of them. Otherwise you wouldn't tremble if one of these is in question. That's why I tell you repeatedly. Practice these things and have them ready at hand - what you should treat with confidence and what with caution. You should be confident about things outside the area of your choice and be cautious towards those that are within. But you say,

"Didn't I read out to you my exercises? Don't you know what I am doing?"

"In what? Your trivial phrases? No. Show me how you deal with desires and aversions to get what you want and avoid what you don't want. As far as your notes, take them away and destroy them."

You may argue that Socrates wrote a lot too. Yes, but for what purpose? He didn't always have someone to test his judgments or to have their judgments tested. He was always trying to examine some preconceived idea or another. That's what he was writing about. He left the trivial phrases to stupid people who didn't understand the logical result of an argument, or to fortunate people who live a life of leisure because of their serenity. Now, when the occasion arises, will you go off reading from your compositions and boast how well you wrote? Don't do it, man.

Free is a person who gets what she desires and not what she doesn't

If you want to boast, do it this way. "Look how I never fail to get what I want and avoid what I don't want. Bring on death, pain, prison, condemnation, and disrepute to me, and you'll know." That's a real test for a young person who has just left the schools. Forget the other stuff. Don't let people ever hear you talk about it. Don't put up with anyone who praises you for it.

Be content to look like a nobody who knows nothing. But show them just this – that you know how to get what you want and avoid what you don't want. Let others study lawsuits, problems, and syllogisms. You should study how to face death, imprisonment, torture, and exile. Do all this with confidence in the one who has called you to face them. He has judged you worthy. Show the superiority of reason over matters where we have no choice. Then the paradox – that we should be confident and cautious at the same time – will no longer be a paradox. Be confident in what does not depend on our choice and be cautious in what does.

Additional Resource

An excellent video on the subject has been posted by Dr Gregory Sadler. To access the video, follow this link: https://goo.gl/G8J1zw

Think about this

For it is not the hardship or death that is a fearful thing, but the fear of hardship or death. Discourses I.1.13. Epictetus [WO]

DISCOURSE 2

Choose Not to Go After External Things

Key ideas of this discourse

1. *When you are the master of your desires and emotions, you win.*
2. *Going after externals makes you a slave.*
3. *Do not provoke others unnecessarily.*

You win when you control your desires and aversions

If you are going to court, consider what you want to keep and what you want to win. If your choice is fully in line with nature, you are totally secure. All will go as planned and you have nothing to worry about. When you guard what is your own and what is by nature free, and want only those things, you don't need to worry about anything. No one else is the master and no one else can take these things away from you. If you want to be a person of honor and trust, who can stop you? If you don't want to be stopped or forced to do something against your will, who is going to make you do it? The judge may pass a sentence which she may think is fearful. But how can she force you to react to it as being terrible? If you control your desires and aversions, there is nothing to worry about. This is your opening statement, your case, and your proof. This is your last word and your acquittal. Therefore, when someone asked Socrates to prepare for the trial, he said

"Don't you think I have been preparing for this my entire life?"

"Preparing for it how?"

"I have minded my own business, never did anything wrong, either in public or in private."

Going after externals makes you a slave

However, if you want to preserve the externals such as your body, property, and reputation, that's a different story. Begin right now. Make every possible preparation. Study the character of the judge and your antagonist. If you must clasp men's knees, clasp them; if you must weep, weep; if you must groan, groan.

When you go after externals you become a slave. Stop being pulled in different directions, wanting to be a slave at one time and wanting to be free at other times. Be one or the other fully: free or a slave, cultivated or ignorant, a fighting cock or a docile one. Endure being beaten to death or give in all at once. You don't want to be the person who withstands many blows and then gives in.

___

Do not provoke, except by intention

If Socrates wanted to preserve externals would he have said, "Anytus and Meletus can kill me but not harm me"? Was he so foolish as not to see this path did not lead to that end, but elsewhere? Why then did he not only disregard the judges, but provoke them as well? Consider what my friend Heraclitus did in a trivial lawsuit about a piece of land in Rhodes. After proving his case, he went on to comment, "I don't care what your decision is going to be. I am not on trial, but *you* are." Thus, he lost his case. What need was there for this?

Don't make any additional comments or even say that you are not going to make any additional comments, unless you want to provoke the judges deliberately, as Socrates did. If you are going to do that, why rise to speak? Why even answer the summons? If you want to be crucified, just wait. The cross will come. But if reason dictates that you should answer the summons and convince the judge to the best of your abilities, you must do accordingly, while always maintaining your true character.

___

There is a price to pay for externals

Looked at this way, it is also ridiculous to say, "Give me some advice." What advice can I give you? You should rather say, "Enable my mind to adapt to whatever happens." To ask for some advice is like asking what name you should write when you are about to print a name. Suppose I say, "Dio," and your teacher comes along and says, "Theo," what will you write? If you have practiced writing, you know what to write no matter what is dictated to you. If you have not, what can I tell you? If conditions suggest something else, what will you say? What will you do?

Remember this general principle and you will need no advice: if you go after externals you will be tossed up and down according to the will of the master. And who is your master? Anyone who has control over what you desire or what you want to avoid.

Think about this

If you gape after externals, you must bob up and down, in obedience to the will of your master. And who is your master? He who has the power over the things which you seek to gain or avoid. Discourses II.2.25-26. Epictetus [GL]

Should You Seek Recommendations?

Key ideas of this discourse

1. *We don't need to seek other people's recommendations. If others can judge us they will do so. If they are not, recommendations won't help anyway.*
2. *We are not able judge life situations correctly because we lack knowledge and experience.*

Others' recommendations are unnecessary

When someone asked Diogenes for a letter of recommendation, he gave him an excellent answer.

"At first glance he will know you are a man. He will also know whether you are good or bad, if he can distinguish the two. But if he doesn't, he will not discover it, even if I write a thousand letters."

Experience and expertise
lead to correct judgement

It is like a coin asking for a recommendation for some person to declare it authentic. If the person in question is an assayer, the coin would speak for itself.

An assayer says, "Bring me any coin you like, I will tell you if it is genuine or a fake." We need a similar skill in life.

I say, "Bring any logical argument to me. I will tell you if it is correct or not." Why? Because I know how to analyze arguments and can judge whether the arguments presented to me are correct or not.

But in life what do I do? I call something good today, bad tomorrow. Why? While I know logic, I lack real life knowledge and experience.

Think about this

Sometimes I call a thing good, and sometimes bad. What is the reason? ... Ignorance and inexperience. Discourses II.3.5. Epictetus [WA]

Choose to Be Faithful

Key ideas of this discourse

1. *We are born to be faithful to one another. Denying this is denying our humanity.*
2. *Even if you are a scholar, if you are not faithful, your humanity is diminished.*

Human beings are born to be faithful

Epictetus was saying that human beings are born to be faithful to one another; denying this is denying our humanity. Just then a scholar, who was found guilty of adultery, happened to walk into the room. Epictetus continued:

If we abandon this natural faithfulness and have designs on our neighbor's wife, what are we really doing? We are ruining and destroying. But whom? The man of trust, principle, and piety. That's not at all. Aren't we also destroying neighborliness, friendship, and community? What position are we putting ourselves in? How am I supposed to treat you now? A neighbor? A friend? What sort of friend? As a citizen? But how can I trust you?

If you were a badly cracked pot that could not be used any more, I would throw you into the garbage. No one would bother to pick you up. But what are we to do with a human who cannot assume a basic human role? If you cannot be a friend, can you at least be a servant? Who would trust you, even in that role? So, like the cracked pot, would you like to be tossed on a dunghill?

Then you will say, "I am a scholar, but no one cares." Yes, because you are a bad and useless human being. It is like wasps protesting that no one respects them and that everyone runs away from them or swats them. Your sting is such that it causes trouble and pain. What do you want us to do? There is no place here where you'll fit in.

'But aren't women meant to be shared?"

"Yes, but only in the sense a roast is shared among guests. But once it is shared, would you steal it from the person seated next to you? Take a piece and taste it? Or dip your finger in the fat and lick it? A fine companion indeed! A dinner guest worthy of Socrates!"

"Isn't the theatre common property?"

"Then maybe you think it is alright to come in when everyone is seated and throw someone out of his seat." [*Zeno, the founder, advocated a community of wives. This radical doctrine was later abandoned, especially by Roman Stoics. Epictetus interprets it differently here.*] Women by nature may be common property. But when they are legally joined, be satisfied to claim your share. Don't grab someone else's."

"But I am a scholar. I understand [the Stoic philosopher] Archedemus."

"So you can. But you are still an adulterer and a cheater. A wolf or an ape rather than a human being. What is there to stop you?"

Think about this

As human beings, we are born to be faithful to one another ... whoever denies this denies their humanity. Discourses. II.4.1. Epictetus [RD]

Choose Only Among Things You Control

Key ideas of this discourse

1. *We have no choice about what happens. But we can choose how to deal with what happens.*
2. *We can be obstructed only in things we don't control.*
3. *Deal only with things under your control. Handle the rest as it comes.*
4. *Be careful how you play ball but be indifferent to the ball itself.*
5. *We are a part of humanity. When we are a part of a larger system, inevitable things happen. Knowing this, deal with things that happen without complaining.*

Imitate dice players when dealing with life

Materials of action are indifferent. But the way we use them is not.

"How, then, can we preserve our stability and peace of mind while, at the same time, taking care to avoid hasty and thoughtless actions?"

"By imitating dice players. The counters are indifferent. So are the players. Our job is to make careful and skillful use of what has fallen, even though we don't know what is going to fall."

Externals are not in our power. Choice is

That's our primary business, even in life. We need to distinguish things, compare them, and understand that, "Externals are not in my power. Choice is."

"Where do I find good and evil?"

"In your choices. In what is your own. When it comes to what belongs to others, never think of anything as good or evil, beneficial or injurious and the like."

"So, can we use externals in a careless way?"

"Not at all. Being careless is an evil when it involves choice. It is unnatural. Care is needed because the *use* of externals is not indifferent. At the same time, we can maintain stability and peace of mind because the externals themselves are indifferent."

We can be obstructed only in matters we don't control

Where something is not indifferent, no one can obstruct and compel us. We can be obstructed or compelled only in matters over which we have no control. These are neither good nor bad, because they are not based on our choices. Blending the two – the carefulness of one devoted to material things with the stability of one who disregards them – may appear difficult, but it is possible. In fact, it is essential for our happiness.

Do what is in your control and deal with the rest as it unfolds

Say you are going on a voyage. What can you do? Whatever is in your power: Pick the captain, the ship, the day, and the time. Then a storm rises. It's no longer your business, it's the captain's. You have done everything you could. Now the ship starts to sink. What can you do now? The only thing you can do – sink. But without fear, without crying, and without accusing God; as one who knows what is born must also die. You are not eternal, but a human being. A part of the whole, as an hour is of the day. An hour ends. So does your life. What difference is there in dying whether it be by drowning or by fever? You must die one way or another.

This is what skillful ballplayers do. They don't consider the ball good or bad but only how to throw it and how to catch it. Grace, skill, speed, and expertise lie in that. While I can't catch their throws even if I spread my coat to do it, they can catch the ball wherever I throw it. But if we are nervous about throwing or catching the ball, there's no fun in it. How can we keep ourselves steady and see what comes next?

"Throw it," says one; "Don't throw it," says another; "You have thrown it already once," says yet another. It would become more a quarrel than a game.

In this sense, Socrates was a ballplayer. He played in the courtroom. He challenged, "Tell me, Anytus, how can you say I don't believe in God? Who do you think are the daemons? Have we not agreed that they are offspring of gods or of gods and humans?'

Anytus agreed.

"Tell me then," Socrates continued, "If someone accepts that there are mules, shouldn't they also accept there are horses and donkeys, the animals that produced them?"

Clearly, Socrates was playing ball. The ball in this case was his life, prison, exile, or execution; being separated from his wife and his children becoming orphans. These were the stakes and yet he played – with skill.

Be careful *how* you play ball, but be indifferent to the ball itself

We need to play the same way: Careful about *how* we play, while being indifferent to the ball itself. We need to show skill in dealing with external materials, without becoming attached them. A weaver does not make the wool but uses her skills on the wool she is given. Whoever has given you food and property can take them back, and your body too. Accept what you are given and work on it.

If you come off unharmed, people who meet you will congratulate you on your escape. But an insightful person will praise you and share your pleasure only if you have acted honorably. He will do the opposite if you have gained your success through dishonest means. When a person has a proper reason to celebrate, others have a reason to join in the celebration.

We are a part of humanity. Inevitably, things happen

Why do we say, then, some externals are natural, while others are not?

It depends on whether we consider them together or separately. For example, if taken by itself, it is natural for my foot to be clean. But if I consider it as a part of my body, then it is proper for my foot to walk through mud and thorns and step on needles. It may even have to be amputated for the sake of the whole body. It cannot be considered a foot otherwise.

We must reason that some such distinction applies to us as well. What are you? A human being. If you think of yourself as a separate unit, then it is natural to live to old age, be wealthy and healthy. But when you think of yourself as a part of humanity, then it is natural for you to get sick, face unsafe situations, struggle to make ends meet and even die before your time.

Why are you then upset? Don't you realize that just as a foot is no longer a foot when detached from the body, you are not a human being when you are detached from humanity? What is a human being? Part of a state. First, the state which is made up of god and humans. Second, the state where one happens to live, which is a small copy of the universal state.

"Why should I be put on trial now? Why do people fall ill, go on an ocean cruise, die or get convicted?"

"We are given such a body as ours, in such a universe as ours, and in such a community as ours. Therefore, what happens to us is unavoidable. It is for you to step forward and deal with these things as best as you can."

Thus, if you are declared guilty, you can tell the judge, "I wish you well. I have done my part. It is for you to decide if you have done yours." After all, don't forget, the judge runs a risk too.

Think about this

Externals are not in my power. Choice is. Where shall I seek good and evil? Within; in what is my own. Discourses. II.5.4-5. Epictetus [CG/RH]

Should You Fear What You Don't Control?

Key ideas of this discourse

1. *Life is indifferent. The way we use it is not.*
2. *When you know less about something, yield to those who know more. On things that you know more than others, don't brag. Minimize your show of superiority.*
3. *Take responsibility for what belongs to you, not for what belongs to others.*
4. *Don't be afraid of what is not under your control.*

Life is indifferent; the way we make use of it is not

Hypothetical arguments are indifferent, but the way you judge them is not indifferent – it can lead to knowledge, or opinion, or delusion. So it is with life – life is indifferent; but the use we make of it is not. Therefore, if someone tells you that these things are indifferent, don't become careless about them; if someone advises you to care about them, don't become miserable or be too impressed by them.

Be gracious when you know more; be yielding when you know less

Have a clear idea about your training and talent in these matters. This way, when you see that you are not qualified, you can keep quiet and not be upset if others outshine you. Where logic is concerned, you can be superior to them. If this upsets them, you can pacify them saying something like, "I just happened to learn these things a few days earlier than you." When something involves practical training, don't pretend you have the skill if you don't have it yet, but yield to those who do. Be content to remain calm and composed.

"Go and pay your compliments to so-and-so."

"Yes, I will. But I won't grovel."

"But you had the door shut on you."

"I have not learned how to break through windows. When I find the door shut I have two options – go away or go through the window."

"Then talk to him."

"I will, but as an equal."

"But you did not get what you wanted."

"That is his business, not mine."

Take responsibility for what belongs to you, not for what belongs to others.

Why take responsibility for something that is not up to you? Always remember what belongs to you and what belongs to others and you won't be disturbed. As Chrysippus said,

"As long as the future is unclear to me, I always hold to those things best adapted to obtaining the things in accordance with nature; for God has created a faculty in me for choosing them. If I knew that my present destiny is to fall ill, I would wish for it. My foot too, if it had intelligence, would choose to get muddy."

Why do grains grow, if not to ripen? Why do they ripen, if not to be harvested? They don't grow for their own sake. If they could talk, would they pray that they are never to be harvested? Would they not consider it a curse instead? Even for humans it is a curse not to die. It is like a wheat grain praying not to ripen or be harvested. Because we are the only animals who not only die but also are aware of dying while it happens, we are upset. This is because we don't know who we are. We don't know what it means to be a human being, unlike a horse trainer who knows what belongs to horses.

Chrysantas [the warrior], was about to strike an opponent down. Just then he heard the trumpet sound a retreat. He immediately pulled back because it was more important for him to obey the commander than follow his own inclinations. Yet, when necessity calls, none of us is ready and willing to obey it. When we do suffer, we don't do so willingly. We cry in protest, and lament "the circumstances." What do you mean by circumstances? If you mean your *personal* circumstances, everything is your personal circumstance. If you mean by circumstances your "troubles," then where is the trouble in something that was born dying? We may be killed by a knife, a torture instrument, the sea, or a tyrant. What difference does it make to us which way we descend into Hades? In truth, no tyrant you fear takes six months to kill you, but a fever you do not fear may kill you over a year. All these things are just noise and empty words.

"My life is at risk when I am with the emperor."

"Do you think I live in less danger here in Nicopolis where earthquakes are common? Aren't you risking your life every time you cross the Adriatic?"

"But even one's opinions can get one into trouble in Rome."

"Your opinions? No one can compel you to hold an opinion against your will. Other peoples' opinions? How can the wrong opinions of others create any danger for you?"

"I also face the danger of being exiled."

"What is exile? Being in a place that is not Rome?"

"Sure. What if I am sent to Gyara?"

"Go to Gyara, if it is worth your while. If not, there is another place you can go to – a place even the person who exiled you is headed, whether he likes it or not."

So why make such a big deal of going to Rome? What is so great about it? Is it worth all this preparation? A gifted young person might say "It has not been worth my while to have listened to so many talks, written so much, and spent so much time next to an old man who is not worth very much himself."

Don't ever lay claim to things that do not belong to you

Just remember the rule that distinguishes what is yours from what is not. Don't ever lay claim to things that do not belong to you. Court and prison are two places, one high, the other low. But, in either place, your choice is the same, if you so decide. When we thus follow Socrates, we can spend time writing hymns in prison.

But, as it stands now, we would hardly have patience with someone who says, "Let me read some hymns of praise to you."

"Why do you bother me? Don't you know the trouble I am in?"

"What trouble?"

"I'm sentenced to die."

"Aren't we all?"

Think about this

Never lay claim to anything that is not your own. Discourses. II.6.24. Epictetus [CG/RH]

Should You Fear the Future?

Key ideas of this discourse

1. *Because we are anxious about the future we go to people like fortune-tellers.*
2. *Even if they can predict the future, they really don't know what is good for us.*
3. *It is best to let things unfold as they do. Whatever happens will be good for us, because everything happens according to God's will.*

No fortune-teller can tell us what is good and evil

We use fortune-tellers when we have no reason to do so. What fortune-teller can see anything worse than death, danger, or illness? If it becomes necessary for me to risk my life for the sake of my friend or even die for him, what occasion is left for me to consult a fortune-teller? Don't I have a true fortune-teller inside of me who has taught me the true nature of good and evil and the signs by which I could know the difference? What use do I have for entrails or birds that are used in fortune-telling? When the fortune-teller says that something will be of benefit to me, should I accept it?

What does he know about what is beneficial to me?

- Does he know what good is?
- Does he know the signs of good and evil, as he does the signs of entrails?

If he knows the signs of good and evil, he also knows what is honorable and shameful and what is just and unjust.

"It is for you (the fortune-teller) to tell me what is in store: life or death, poverty or wealth. But about whether they are beneficial or harmful, am I going to ask you? You don't speak on points of grammar, do you? And yet, here you are, presuming to speak on matters on which we all go astray and can never agree."

A woman wanted to send a boatload of provisions to a senator's exiled wife Gratilla. When someone said to her, "What's the use? The Emperor Domitian would confiscate them anyway," she gave an excellent reply. "I would rather have them confiscated than my not sending them at all."

It's our fear that leads us to consult fortune-tellers

Why then do we consult fortune-tellers so often? Cowardice. Our fear of what may happen. So, we flatter the fortune-tellers:

"Please, sir, will I inherit my father's property?"

"Let's see. We must offer a sacrifice about that matter."

"Yes sir, as fortune wills."

"You will inherit your father's property."

If he says that, we thank him profusely as if it his property we are inheriting. What happens as a result? They go on deceiving us.

God wants the best for us. Let everything happen as it does.

How should we approach them then? We should go to them without desire or aversion, like a traveler who reaches a fork on the road, not knowing which road to take. She doesn't have any preference as to which road she takes, if it is the one that will take her to where she wants to go. We should also use God as a guide in the same way, like we use our eyes. We don't ask our eyes to accept only particular impressions, but all that eyes can show us.

Instead, we approach fortune-tellers as if they were gods, imploring them to tell us good news.

You want what is best for you. Now, what is best for you other than what God wishes? Why do you then do everything possible to corrupt your judge, to mislead your counsellor?

Think about this

What, then, leads us to consult diviners so constantly? Cowardice, our fear of what will turn out. Discourses. II.7.9. Epictetus [CG/RH]

Choose to Look After Your Inherent Qualities

Key ideas of this discourse

1. *The nature of God is in knowledge and right reason.*
2. *Plants and animals cannot interpret the impressions they receive. So, we cannot apply the terms "good" and "bad" to them.*
3. *Humans are the principal work of God and they can interpret the impressions they receive.*
4. *God is within us all the time, but we are not aware of it.*
5. *God wants us to look after ourselves and preserve the qualities we are born with: modesty, faithfulness, dignity, patience, calmness, and poise.*
6. *We will not be able to avoid death and disease, but we can bear death and disease with godlike dignity.*

39

The true nature of God

God is helpful. What is good is also helpful. It seems then that where there is the true nature of God, there is also is the true nature of good.

"What, then, is the true nature of God. Is it flesh?"

"Certainly not!"

"Land? Status?"

"Not at all."

The nature of God is in knowledge and right reason. Only here should you look for the true nature of good. You won't find it in plants or animals. Then why go looking for it in places other than what distinguishes the rational from the irrational?

The terms "good' and "evil" do not apply to plants or animals

The terms "good' and "evil" do not apply to plants because they don't have the capacity to deal with external impressions. Even the ability to deal with external impressions is not enough. If it is, then you should be able to speak of "good," "happy," and "unhappy," when we talk about animals as we do when we talk about humans. But we don't, for a good reason.

Animals may use external impressions well but cannot reflect on them or understand them. Why? Because animals are created to serve, and they do not have any other primary purpose. A donkey was created because humans needed an animal with a strong back that could carry a heavy load. Because the donkey also needed to walk around, it was given the ability to deal with external impressions for this purpose. But that's where it ends. If donkeys had the ability to go further and understand how to deal with impressions, they would refuse to obey us and would be our equal. And rightly so.

Humans are the principal works of God

"Because the nature of good is absent from both plants and animals, should you not look for it in that quality that distinguishes humans from all other things?"

"Aren't plants and animals works of God?"

"They are. But they are not of primary importance and are not parts of God."

But you are a principal work of God, a fragment of Him. You have a part of Him in you. Why are you then ignorant of your noble birth? Why don't you remember your origin? Why don't you remember, when you eat, who you are and whom you are feeding? When you have sex, who is it that's doing it? Whenever you converse, exercise, or socialize, don't you know that it is with God you do these things?

God is always with us and we don't know it

You carry God around you and you don't know it, poor fool! I am not talking about some external god made of silver or gold. The god you carry around with you is a living one and yet you are so blind to the fact that you defile Him with your impure thoughts and offensive behavior. You wouldn't repeat such behavior even when a god's statue is nearby. When God himself is there within you, and sees and hears everything you do and say, are you not ashamed to think and act the way you do? You are not aware of your own nature and are an object of God's anger.

What are we anxious about when we send out a young man into the real world after he graduates from school? That he may make mistakes, eat poorly, have affairs, humiliate himself, and dress in poor clothes or dress to impress? Why? Because he is ignorant that God is within him. He fails to realize who goes with him and says, "I wish you were here with me." Is it not so that God is with him wherever he goes? Having Him with you, why look for someone else? Would they tell you any different?

If you were a sculpture made by [the famous sculptor] Phidias, then you would have remembered who you are and who it is that made you. If you had any intelligence, you would try to avoid doing anything unworthy of your creator or of you, such as making yourself a spectacle in front of others. God made you. Are you then unconcerned about the spectacle you make of yourself? How can you even compare the creations of a sculptor with creations of God?

What other work of art comes with all the powers that the artist displayed while making it? Is it anything more than marble, bronze, gold, or ivory? Phidias' statue of Athena, once finished with its arms raised to support Victory, remains that way forever. The works of God, on the other hand, are living, breathing beings. They can deal with impressions and test them. When you are the work of such an artist, will you discredit him – especially when he not only created you but has given you complete control over yourself? You not only forget that but dishonor the trust he placed in you.

God has entrusted each one of us to our own care

If God had asked you to care for some orphans, would you have ignored them? God has asked you to care for yourself, saying, "I don't have anyone more dependable than you. Preserve this person for me along with the qualities nature has given him: modesty, faithfulness, dignity, patience, calmness, and poise." Will you not keep him so?

People might say, "Why does this person look so serious and self-important?"

"Well that's only because I am not yet totally confident about the principles I have learned and agreed to live by. I am still afraid of my weakness. Let me gain more confidence and I will show you the right look and bearing. I will show you what a completed and polished statue looks like."

What do you think of it? A proud look? Heaven forbid! Even God doesn't have a proud look. He keeps up the steady gaze of a person who is about to say, "My words are irrevocable and true." I will show you that I am the kind of person who is faithful, honorable, noble, and poised.

We can all be godlike

"Do you mean to say that you are immune from illness, death, age, and disease?"

"No, but I would die and bear disease godlike. This much is in my power. This I can do. All other things you say are not in my power and I cannot do them. I will show you the strength of a philosopher."

"What kind of strength are you talking about?"

"A desire that is always fulfilled. An aversion that does not face what it wants to avoid. The right choice. A well-considered assent. This is what you shall see."

Think about this

[Strengths of a philosopher]: *Desire that never fails in its achievement; aversion that never meets with what it wants to avoid; appropriate impulse; carefully considered purpose; and assent that is never precipitate. This is what you shall see.* Discourses I.8.29. Epictetus [CG/RH]

Choose to Act on Your Knowledge

Key ideas of this discourse

1. *Each person or thing is strengthened and preserved by actions that reflect its nature: Modesty is preserved by modest actions, and trustworthiness is preserved by trustworthy behavior.*

2. *Each person or thing is weakened and destroyed by actions that are contrary to its nature: Modesty is destroyed by shamelessness, and trustworthiness is destroyed by untrustworthy behavior.*

3. *Over time, we start behaving in a way that is contrary to what we learned.*

4. *We are quick to recite the principles of Stoicism but don't live by them.*

5. *This is because we are trying to be a philosopher when we can barely fulfil the role of a human being.*

How human beings are preserved and destroyed

It is not easy to fulfil our role as human beings.

"What is a human being?"

"A rational, mortal animal."

"What does our rational nature distinguish us from?"

"From wild animals and animals like sheep."

"Then take care not act like sheep and thus destroy your humanity. When we act to satisfy our gluttony and sexual desires, when our actions are random, dirty, and thoughtless, to what level have we sunk?"

"To that of wild beasts."

Some of us are large wild beasts. Others are small animals, little evil-natured creatures, which make us say, "I would rather be eaten by a lion."

All such actions destroy our calling as human beings.

A complex thing is preserved when it fulfils its functions and its various parts are true to their nature. A discrete thing is preserved when it fulfils its function. When are flutes, a lyre, a horse, a dog preserved? Why then, are we to be surprised if humans are preserved the same way and destroyed the same way?

Everything is strengthened and preserved by actions that reflect its nature

Each person is strengthened and preserved by actions that reflect his nature: A carpenter by the art of carpentry, a grammar expert by grammatical studies. If the grammar expert starts writing ungrammatically, his art will be destroyed. Modesty is preserved by modest actions but destroyed by shameless ones; trustworthiness is preserved by trustworthy behavior while behavior contrary to it destroys it.

Acts of opposite character preserves the opposite character. Shamelessness by shameless behavior, dishonesty by dishonest behavior, slanderousness by slander, a bad temper by anger, and miserliness by disproportionate taking compared to giving.

This why we shouldn't be content just to learn, but add practice, followed by training. Over time, we get into the habit of doing the opposite of what we learn and use opinions that are the opposite of correct ones. So, unless we apply the correct opinions, we will just be interpreting other people's judgments.

Anyone can talk the talk

We can all talk the talk: What is good and evil? Some things are good, some evil, and others indifferent. Virtues and things related to them are good. Evil is the opposite. Indifferents are things like health, wealth, and reputation.

Then we are interrupted. There is a loud noise. Someone laughs at us. We are immediately upset! Tell me, philosopher, what happened to the things you were just talking about? Where was it coming from? Your lips. That's all. Then, why do you pervert helpful thoughts that are not yours? Why do you gamble with important things?

Can you walk the walk?

Storing wine and bread in your pantry is one thing, eating them is another. What you eat is digested and distributed around your body and it becomes sinews, flesh, bones, blood, a good complexion, and easy breathing. What is stored away is ready and available for display whenever you choose. But you get no benefit from it, except a reputation for owning it.

So, what difference does it make whether you talk about the teachings of this school or some other school? Maybe you will give a better account of the teachings of Epicurus than Epicurus himself! Why call yourself a Stoic and deceive others? Why act the part of a Jew when you are a Greek? Don't you know the reason a person is called a Jew, a Syrian, or an Egyptian? When someone wavers between two faiths, we say, "He is no Jew. He is just acting the part." But once he makes his choice and assumes the attitude of one who is baptized, he is really a Jew and we call him one. So also, we are fake Baptists; Jews in name only, but something quite different. We do not follow our principles but are proud we know them.

Don't try to be a philosopher when you can barely be a human being

We take on the role of a philosopher when we can barely fulfil the role of a human being, even though it is a massive burden. It is like a person who can't lift ten pounds wanting to lift the rock of Ajax!

Think about this

Modest acts preserve the modest man, whereas immodest acts destroy him; and faithful acts preserve the faithful man while acts of the opposite character destroy him. Discourses I.9. *** Epictetus [WO]

Choose to Play Your Different Roles Well

Key ideas of this discourse

1. *You have distinct roles to play: a human being, a citizen, a father or a mother, a son or a daughter, and a brother or a sister.*

2. *You should act in a way that is consistent with your role. For example, if you are a brother, check to see if your actions are consistent with your role as a brother.*

3. *When you don't play your role in a way that is appropriate to that role, you lose your character.*

4. *Unfortunately, a loss of character is not accompanied by illness or loss of property. So, you don't even realize what you have lost.*

5. *If someone hurts us, they pay a penalty because they injure themselves. If we try to hurt them in return, we injure ourselves.*

6. *Develop character with a view to making the right choice, not for show in a debating forum.*

Who are you?

You are a human being

First, you are a human being. Your highest quality is the power to choose. Everything else you have is subject to that, but the power to choose itself is unrestrained and absolute. The second quality you possess is your power to reason which separates you from wild animals and animals like sheep.

You are a citizen of the world

The two faculties – power to choose and reason – make you a citizen of the world. You are a principal part of it, not a subsidiary. No part of the world is designed to serve because all of them are of primary importance. You understand how the world is governed and what follows from it.

What does it mean to be a citizen? It means not acting for purely personal gains, detached from the interests of the society, just like a foot or hand. If your body organs had the rational faculty, they would not choose to act in any other way except with reference to the whole body. Therefore, philosophers say, "If a good person knew disease, death, or disability is in store for him, he would actually welcome them. He would realize that it is part of the universal plan. The universe is more important than the part, and the state is more important than any citizen." But since we don't know the future, we should choose things that are preferable by nature, because we are born for this purpose.

You are someone's son/daughter

You are someone's son or daughter. In this role, consider what you have also belongs to your father. Obey him, do not hurt him by words or deeds or complain about him. Yield to him and cooperate with him to the best of your ability.

You are someone's brother/sister

In your role as someone's brother/sister, be respectful, ready to yield, and gracious. Do not fight over material things, things over which you have no control. Give them up cheerfully so you may have a larger share of things over which you do have control. The cost of the material thing you give up – whether it is food or some furniture – is nothing compared to the goodwill you gain in return.

Remember your role as you play it

If you are a council member, remember the duties of a councilor; if young, duties of the young; if old, duties of the old; and, if a father, duties of a father. When you consider your title as you play distinct roles, it will become obvious what you are expected to do. Thus, if you speak ill of your brother, I say to you, "You have forgotten who you are as a brother." If you are a metalworker and cannot use a hammer properly, then you have forgotten your skill as a metal worker. It is no trivial matter if you become your brother's enemy, forgetting what it means to be a brother. If you – instead of being gentle and social – have become a dangerous wild animal ready to bite, do you think you have lost nothing? Or do you have to lose money before you feel you lost something? Is that the only loss that counts?

Do not lose your character

If you lost your skill in language or music, you would consider it a big loss. Yet you seem to think it is a trivial matter to lose your ability to be honest, gentle, and dignified. Abilities in language and music come from external causes. There is no shame in not having them or losing them. But losing your positive traits is your own fault. Not having positive traits, or losing them once having had them, is shameful, dishonorable, and worthy of rebuke.

There is no one who is bad and doesn't pay the penalty. A victim of unnatural lust loses the man in him. So does the man who uses him, besides many other things. An adulterer loses self-respect, self-control, and good behavior; his ability to be a good citizen and neighbor. An angry person loses something, a fearful person something else. They may not have lost in terms of money and may even stand to gain by such behavior. But if you reduce everything to money, you might think that someone who loses his nose does not suffer any harm.

"Yes, they do. They lost something physical."

"But what about something psychological, such as the sense of smell? What about a faculty which is beneficial if you had it but injurious if you didn't?"

"What faculty do you mean?"

"Don't we have a sense of fairness?"

"Yes, we do."

"If you destroy it, have you not suffered any harm? Not sacrificed anything? Not lost something that belonged to you? Don't we have a natural sense of affection, helpfulness, and compassion? If you carelessly allow yourself to lose these qualities, would you consider yourself unharmed and undamaged?"

"Why shouldn't I harm someone who harmed me?"

"Think about what philosophers said about what "harm" is. If good and evil is the result of our choice, is this not what you are saying: "Since he hurt himself by harming me, shouldn't I also hurt myself by harming him?"

Understand what you lose when you lose your character

Why don't we put it like this to ourselves? When our body or possessions are involved, we see harm. But when our choices are involved, we don't see any harm at all. After all, if we have been deceived or if we have done something wrong, we don't get a headache, or lose our eyes or hips or lose our property. We are not interested in anything beyond these. We don't care whether our choice is honest and trustworthy or shameless and untrustworthy, except as a topic of trivial classroom debate. So, we make some progress in terms of our debating skills but not in terms of our character.

Think about this

No one becomes bad without suffering loss or damage.
Discourses II.7.10. Epictetus [RH]

Have Standards to Evaluate Your Principles

Key ideas of this discourse

1. We have an innate sense of good and evil, honorable, and dishonorable, appropriate, and inappropriate.
2. But this innate sense is not enough to apply these principles in specific cases, because different people see these things differently.
3. We cannot go by our intuition either. It also varies from person to person.
4. Therefore, we look up to philosophy which establishes standards by which you can judge the correctness of a proposition, which we should all follow.

We need to learn
how to apply concepts to real life

When you come to study philosophy the right way, you begin by acknowledging your weakness with reference to important things in life.

We are not born with the knowledge of what a right-angled triangle is or with an understanding of what a half-tone scale in music interval is. We were trained to learn them. Those who are not so trained do not pretend that they know about these concepts.

We all agree on principles,
but not on how to apply them

Has anyone come into this world without having an innate concept of what is good and evil, honorable, and dishonorable, appropriate, and inappropriate, happiness, duty, and obligation? So, everyone applies these concepts to specific situations. We hear things like this all the time: "He has done well," "She has been unfortunate," "She is a bad woman," or "He is just a man." We don't doubt the meaning of these words or stop ourselves from using them. We don't wait until we are taught their meaning, like we do when we deal with concepts relating to subjects like geometry or music. Why? Because we are born with some understanding of these concepts and to this we add our own interpretation.

"Do you mean to say that I have no idea about what is good and evil?"

"Yes, you do."

"Can't I apply this knowledge to specific instances?"

"Yes, you can."

"I apply it rightly then."

Something does not become correct just because we think so

"Ah, not exactly. Our opinions become an issue here. We all start with agreed-upon principles, but we get into disputes because we apply them incorrectly. If you knew how to apply them correctly, then there would be no problem. Since you say that you can apply these principles correctly, tell me, how do you know it?"

"It feels right."

"But someone else feels something else is right. So, she feels she is correct in the way *she* applies the principles. Right?"

"Yes."

"You cannot both be applying the principles correctly, if you have different opinions."

"Agreed."

"So, you need to show me something more than your feeling that you are right. For a lunatic, what he does seems right. Would you say, then, that it is sufficient?"

"No."

"So, we need to move beyond our opinion."

"What is that?"

We need a standard
to decide whether something is right

This is the beginning of philosophy: We note that people disagree in their opinion. We want to understand why this is so. In doing so, we don't rely on simple opinion but look for a way to decide whether the opinion is right or wrong. We want to have a standard of judgment – a standard like a balance for judging weights or a carpenter's rule to judge whether something is crooked or straight – to see if it is the correct opinion.

"How can 'what everyone thinks is right,' be the beginning of philosophy when people have conflicting opinions?"

"Then are our opinions correct?"

"Why ours rather than those of Syrians or Egyptians? Why mine rather than someone else's?"

"There is no reason why."

So, we cannot establish something is correct just because it feels correct to us. It is not enough evidence. Even in weights and measures, we are not content judging things by appearance. Rather we use standardized weights. So, we ask, don't we have any higher standard in this case than our opinion? How is it possible that something so important in human life is incapable of determination and discovery?

It is clear then that there is some standard. Why don't we then find it and, after finding it, use it forever without fail, and do not as much stretch out a finger without it? This will get rid of the madness that comes from thinking that our opinion is the truth. We will start with well-known and clearly defined principles and apply them to specific cases.

"What do you want to talk about now?'

"Pleasure."

"All right. Put it to the test, put it into the balance. If it is good, we should be able to rely on it and put our trust in it. It should be stable."

"Agreed."

"Is pleasure stable?"

"No."

"Then throw it out. Take it away from things that are good. But if you are not quick enough to see this and one test is not enough for you, let us try a different one. Shouldn't something good be a source of happiness?"

"Yes."

"Can a momentary pleasure really bring happiness? And don't say yes. If you did, I 'd say you are not worthy of using the scale."

This is how things are judged and measured when philosophy establishes standards. Wise and good people make it their business to make use of these standards.

Think about this

[The] opinion each person holds is not enough criterion for determining the truth. Discourses II.11.16. Epictetus [RH]

Choose the Right Way to Argue

Key ideas of this discourse

1. *It is important that our arguments are logical.*
2. *However, we don't know how to argue logically. We confuse ourselves and others, become abusive, and walk away.*
3. *Socrates taught us how to do it right: Don't use complicated words; be patient; don't ever get angry or abusive, even if your opponent is.*
4. *But remember, it may not be a clever idea to argue with everyone, even if you are right.*

We are not good at logical arguments

Stoic philosophers have told us what exactly we must learn to argue logically. But we have no experience at all in applying it correctly. If we are given someone random to argue with, we won't know how to deal with him. If he continues to challenge us after a little while, we resort to abuse or ridicule saying, "He is just a layperson. It's not possible to have a proper dialog with him."

If a guide finds someone who has lost his way, she would not ridicule or abuse him or walk away from him but show him the right path. So, it is your job to show the other person the right path and you will see that he follows it. But if you have not done this, don't make fun of him but recognize that you have not done your part. [This confidence that people follow the wrong path only because of their ignorance but will change once you show them the right way, runs through Epictetus' writings.]

Use plain language anyone can understand

Here is how Socrates acted. He would force the person he is talking with to be his witness and he needed no other. He could say, "I don't care for others, but only for the person I am talking with. No one else's vote counts except his." Socrates then would make the implications of their views so clearly that everyone would see the how contradictory their arguments are and abandon them.

"Is an envious person happy because he is envious?"

"No, they are miserable."

Socrates moved the person into admitting envy does not make him happy.

"Is envy being miserable at something bad? How can anyone envy something that's bad?"

Now Socrates has moved his opponent into admitting that envy is feeling pain at something good.

"Does anyone envy things that don't matter to them?"

"No, not at all."

As soon as his opponent comes to a different understanding, Socrates would quit.

Socrates wouldn't ask his opponent to define envy and then try to correct him. After all, these terms are technical and complicated, and it is hard for a layperson to follow, but we cannot resist using them. We don't know to use plain language that any layperson could understand and answer with a simple yes or no. When we realize that we are unable to express ourselves clearly, we give up, especially those of us who are cautious. But most of us are not. So, we persist, confuse ourselves and others, exchange abuses, and then walk away.

Never lose your cool

Socrates was well-known for remaining unprovoked in an argument and not being abusive even when insulted; he would be patient with the opponent and put an end to the conflict. Would you like to know how good he was at this? Then read Xenophon's *Symposium*. You'll see how many disputes he ended. Even poets praised this quality of his with these words:

"He could cut short a dispute, however great, with his skill."

Be careful who you argue with

Engaging in logical dialogs is not a safe business any more, especially in Rome. If you pursue logic, you cannot do it in a corner. You find someone rich and powerful and ask him:

"Sir, do you know who is looking after your horses?"

"I do."

"Is it the first person who came along, whether he knew anything about horses or not?"

"Of course not."

"What about your money? Your clothes?"

"No, I don't hand over these to the first person who comes along."

"Do you have someone who looks after your body?'

"Yes, of course."

"I presume to an expert in exercise and medicine?"

"Yes."

"Are these the things you value most, or do you have something even better?"

"What do you mean?"

"The faculty that uses, tests, and thinks about all these things."

"You mean my soul?"

"Exactly. That's what I mean."

"Absolutely. It is by far the best thing I possess. Better than all other things."

"Then tell me how you take care of your soul. Surely someone as wise and respected as you are would not neglect and ruin the most precious thing you have?"

"Certainly not."

"Do you take care of it yourself? If so, did you learn how from someone else or did you discover it yourself?"

At this point, you are entering the danger zone with the other person responding with, "How is this your business? Are you my boss?" If you persist, he may punch you in the face. I am speaking from experience. I used to be keen on such discourses – until I met with such troubles.

Think about this

When a guide meets us with someone who is lost, ordinarily his reaction is to direct him on the right path, not mock or malign him. Discourses II.12.3. Epictetus [RD]

Choose Knowledge over Anxiety

Key ideas of this discourse

1. *When you feel anxious about meeting someone, it is because you believe they have something that you want, and you may not get it.*

2. *This arises out of your ignorance about what is under your control and what is not. Once you study this fully and understand it, you will not feel anxious under any condition.*

3. *If you still think others can control you and feel anxious about it, then you have not understood what I have been telling you. You are not cut out to be a philosopher.*

The reason for anxiety is ignorance

Whenever I see someone who is anxious, I ask, "What does this person want?" Unless you want something that is not under your control, how can you be anxious? If you play a musical instrument by yourself, you have no anxiety. But when you enter a music hall, even if you have a fine voice and can play the instrument well, you become anxious. You not only want to sing well but also want to be applauded by listeners, which is not under your control.

"Where you have knowledge, there you have confidence and you are not concerned about what others may think. So, your anxiety comes from lack of knowledge and practice in areas other than music."

"Lack of knowledge and practice about what?"

"You don't understand what an audience is or what their applause means. You have learned how to play all the notes from the lowest to the highest. But what an audience is, what its applause amounts to – this you have not studied or understood. So, you necessarily become nervous and pale."

I can't say that you are not a musician just because you are nervous, but I can say many other things about you. I call you a stranger because you don't understand where you are living; you have lived here all your life yet do not understand the laws and customs of the country. You don't know what is permitted and what is not. You have not consulted a lawyer who could tell you how things work here.

STOIC CHOICES • 71

Where there is knowledge, there is no anxiety

No one writes a will without knowing how to write it or consulting someone who does; or sign a bond and offer guarantees. But when it comes to desire, aversion, impulse, intention, and purpose, we don't care about consulting an expert.

"Why do you say that?"

"Because people want what they cannot have and try to avoid what they cannot escape. They do not know what belongs to them and what belongs to others. For, if they did know all this, they would not be blocked or disappointed. Or anxious."

"Why?"

"Do you fear something that's not bad or evil?"

"No."

"Or things you have the power to avoid, even if they are bad and evil?"

"Of course, not."

"So, if things outside our control are neither good nor bad and things that we control cannot be taken away from us, or imposed on us without our consent, then what is left for us to be anxious about?"

What are we anxious about? Our body, our possessions, and what powerful people may do to us. Never about anything under our control. Are we anxious about having a false opinion? No, because it is under our control. Are we anxious about falling for an unnatural desire? Again, no, because this is under our control. So, if you see someone pale and anxious, just like a doctor diagnosing trouble from a patient's skin, say, "He is affected by desires and aversions and is not well. Because nothing else can account for his change in complexion, his trembling, his chattering teeth, or his shifting weight from one knee to another."

Therefore, when he went to see [the emperor] Antigonus, Zeno [the founder of Stoicism] had no anxiety. What Zeno valued, the emperor had no power over. Things that the emperor had power over weren't the things that Zeno valued. But the emperor was anxious about meeting Zeno because he wanted to please Zeno, which was out of his control. Zeno had no great desire to please the emperor. Why would an expert need approval from a rookie? For what? Do you know the standards by which someone can be judged? What a good or a bad person is and how they got that way? If so, how come you are not a good person yourself?

"How do you figure that?"

"Because good people do not grieve, complain, or groan. They don't turn pale, tremble, and say, "How will he receive me? Will he listen to me?" Idiot, it is his concern. He will do as he pleases. Why do you worry about things that are not your business? If he fails to receive you well, is it not *his* problem?"

"Sure."

"Is it possible that someone makes a mistake and someone else suffers the harm?"

"No. But I am still anxious about how I will talk to him."

"Why can't you talk to him anyway you like."

"I am afraid I will lose my composure."

"If I were to write the name "Dion," would you be anxious?"

"No."

"And why not? Is it not because you have learned how to write it?"

"Yes."

"And would you be as confident reading the name?"

"Yes."

"Because when you study a discipline, you gain strength and confidence in that discipline. Now you have practice in speaking. What else did they teach you at school?"

"Logic and arguments that change."

"For what reason if not to argue skillfully? 'Skillfully' meaning to argue with polish, and argue securely, intelligently, without being flustered or confused easily, and with confidence."

"Yes."

"Then you are like a soldier on horse-back about to meet a foot-soldier. Are you still anxious?"

"But the king has the power to kill me."

"Then speak the truth, sorry specimen, and don't brag or call yourself a philosopher. Be aware who your masters are and, as long as you allow them to control you through your body, be ready to submit to anyone stronger than you."

True philosophers are not anxious

Socrates had studied how to speak. So, he spoke the way he did to tyrants, to the jury, and to anyone when in prison. Diogenes had studied how to speak. So, he spoke the way he did to Alexander, to Philip, to the pirates, and to the person to whom the pirates sold him as a slave. As for you, just leave these to those who have studied the matter and are confident. Return to your own business and just be there. Make up syllogisms and explain them to others. "In you, the state has found no captain."

Think about this

If you have this attachment to your body, be ready to submit to anyone or anything of superior physical force. Discourses II.13.23. Epictetus [RD]

Choose to Align Your Desires with Reality

Key ideas of this discourse

1. *The learning process is difficult. While the results are pleasing, the practice is monotonous.*
2. *The practice of a philosopher is to bring his desires in line with whatever happens. Nothing can happen against his will, so his life is free from sorrow, fear, and disturbance.*
3. *We should be like the gods in being free, benevolent, and compassionate.*
4. *Most people go through life mechanically without wonder. You should develop a curiosity about the festival of life.*

Pleasing results are the result of monotonous practice

A visitor from Rome [presumably a well-known person, Julius Naso] came with his son to see Epictetus. At one of his lectures, Epictetus said, "This is the way I teach," and then stopped talking. When the visitor requested Epictetus to continue, he replied, "The learning process is always difficult for those who are new to an art and not familiar with it."

Most finished products are attractive and charming, and their use is obvious. It may not be a joy to watch the way a shoemaker learns his art, but nevertheless the shoes he makes are useful, and aesthetically pleasing. The way a carpenter learns his trade may be tedious to watch, but what he produces turns out to be useful. This is even truer of music. If you watch someone learning music, you will find it quite monotonous. Yet the final product is pleasing and entertains everyone.

Bring your desires in line with whatever happens

Similarly, a philosopher's job goes something like this: He must bring his desires in line with whatever happens, so nothing ever happens against his will and nothing fails to happen except as he wishes. If you follow this, nothing will ever happen against your will and nothing will fail to happen except as you wish. You will lead a personal life free from sorrow, fear, and disturbance. At the same time, you will nourish your roles, whether it is natural or acquired, as a son, father, brother, citizen, wife, fellow-traveler, ruler or ruled.

Use your divine nature as your model

How do we achieve this? If you want to be a carpenter or a pilot, you need some formal training. It is the same here as well. It is not enough to wish to become wise and good, we need to learn certain things. We must find out what they are. The philosophers tell us that we should first learn that there is a God and that He provides for the Universe. We cannot keep our actions – or even our intentions and thoughts – hidden from Him.

Then we must learn about the divine nature. If we want to please the gods, we must obey them and try to resemble them to the best of our ability. If the divine nature is trustworthy, we should be trustworthy; if the divine nature is free, benevolent, and compassionate, we should be free, benevolent, and compassionate as well. We should use God as our model for our thoughts and behavior.

"Where do I begin, then?"

"First start by understanding the meaning of words."

"Do you mean to say that I don't understand them now?"

"Yes, I do."

"How is it, then, I have been using them?"

"Like the way illiterate people use written signs, or the way cattle use their senses. Using something is different from understanding it. But if you really think that you understand the words you use, let's start with a few and test them to see whether we understand them or not."

"I am a grown man and have been to three wars. I don't appreciate being tested like this now."

"Don't I know it? You are here not because you think you need to learn anything. You cannot even imagine what you could possibly need. You are rich, probably have a wife, and many servants. The king himself knows you, you have many friends, you perform your duties, and you know how to reward your friends and punish your enemies. What more could you want?"

The missing element: The key to happiness

What if I could show you that you are missing the key to happiness? That you have spent all these days on things that are not right for you? That, to top it all, you don't know what god is, what a human being is, and what good and evil are? If I say you are ignorant of these things, you may bear with me. But, if I add that you don't even know who you are, how can you tolerate it? Will you be patient, put up with my questioning and stay with me? Not at all. You'll be offended and leave immediately.

Yet, what harm have I done to you? None. No more than a mirror that shows a plain person for what she looks like. Or a doctor who tells the patient, "Do you think you are well? No, you are sick. Don't eat anything today. Just drink water." No one says, "How rude!" But if I say to anyone "Your desires are unhealthy, your attempts to avoid things are humiliating, your purposes are confused, your choices are at odds with nature, and your values are random and false," he immediately walks out saying, "Epictetus insulted me."

Most people don't pay attention to the festival of life

This is like what happens when you attend a fair where cattle are bought and sold. Most people are there to buy and sell cattle. But there a few who come just to see how the fair is organized, who is promoting it and why. The "fair" of the world in which we live is no different. Some people, like cattle, care only for their food. Your possessions, property, large household with servants, and public status are nothing more than cattle fodder.

A few others who attend the fair are capable of reflecting, "What is this world? Who runs it? No one?" No city or a house can function even briefly without someone taking care of it. And can this design, so vast and so beautiful, run on its own, by mere chance? Therefore, there must be somebody who governs it. But who is he? How does he govern? What are we who were made by him? What purpose are we here to fulfil? Are we connected to him or not? They think about these things, make time for this, and learn as much as possible about the festival of life before they leave the fair.

The result? They are laughed at by others, just as spectators would be laughed at by traders. And as cattle would laugh at those who are interested in anything other than fodder, if they had any understanding.

Think about this

What if I were to show you that all that's missing are the keys to happiness? That your life has been devoted to everything except what it ought to be? Discourses II.14.19. Epictetus [RD]

Base Your Decisions on Sound Foundation

Key ideas of this discourse

1. *Some people make decisions and stand by them, because they believe standing by their decision is the right thing to do.*
2. *However, standing by one's decision is good only if the decisions are based on a sound foundation.*
3. *Standing by unexamined decisions is a form of sickness. If you become stubborn about unexamined decisions, you are beyond help.*

Don't cling to high-sounding but unexamined decisions

Some people, when they hear principles like

- You should be unwavering,
- Choice by nature is free and cannot be restrained, and

- Everything else is unfree, can be restrained and is not under our control,

assume that they should stand by their interpretation of such principles and not give in, even a bit.

No, the first thing is to make sure that the decision is a sound one. I would like a body that's strong, strength that comes out of good health and training. If your strength comes out the frenzy of a madman and if you boast about that, then I would say, "Get yourself a therapist. This is not strength but quite the opposite."

Here is another way in which people misinterpret the principles. A friend of mine decided to starve himself to death for no reason. I came to know about this on the third day of his fast and went to see him and asked him.

"Why are you starving yourself to death?"

"Because I have made my decision."

"True. If it is the right decision, we will stand by you and help you in your passage. But if it is irrational, you should change it."

"We must stick with a decision."

"That applies only to a sound decision, not to any decision. If you imagine that this is night (when it is day), would you believe then that it must be true, and you should not change your mind?"

Decisions should stand on strong foundations

Start with a solid foundation at the beginning. Examine your decisions to see if they are correct. If it is, then and only then, do you have the basis for a firm resolve. If your foundation is rotten and crumbling, you cannot build even a small building on that. If you attempt to build a larger and heavier one, it would collapse even faster.

You are taking the life of my old friend, with whom I share this universe and this city, even though he has not done anything wrong. This is an act of murder and you say that you must stand by your decision. If the idea to kill me ever entered your mind, would you stand by that decision too?

Unexamined decisions are a sickness

It was demanding work, persuading him to change his mind. But there are some people these days who cannot be persuaded at all. Now I understand the meaning of the proverb, (which I didn't understand before) "A fool you can neither bend nor break." I hope I never have a clever fool for a friend.

"I have decided!" he says.

So do crazy people. The more delusional they are, the more medication they need. Do what sick people do. Call a doctor and tell him, "Doctor, I am sick. Help me. I will accept whatever you prescribe."

You will do something similar in this case. "I don't know what I should be doing. I have come to you to find out." But instead you say, "My mind is made up about this. Talk about something else." What "something else?" What is more important and more helpful to you than making you understand that it is not enough to arrive at a decision and refuse to change it? This is crazy, not healthy.

"I intend to die, even though I don't have to."

"Why, man? What's the matter?"

"I have decided."

"It's lucky for me that you have not decided to kill me!"

Someone else says, "I won't take any money for my services."

"Why man? What's the matter?"

"I have decided."

"I am positive that someday you would change your mind, start accepting money, and declare equally passionately, 'I have decided!' What's there to stop it?"

Your sickness of mind is like that of sickness of a body, with sickness showing up in various parts of the body at various times. When you add strength of purpose to this sickness, it gets past help and healing.

Think about this

"But we must stick with a decision."

"For heaven's sake, man, that rule applies only for sound decisions."

Discourses II.15.7, Epictetus [RD]

Our Choices Give Rise to Good and Evil

Key ideas of this discourse

1. *All good and evil arise out of the choices we make.*

2. *You will stop being fearful once you understand the nature of praise and blame.*

3. *We are given the gift of endurance, nobility, and courage. Let's use them to solve our problems and stop complaining.*

4. *Always remember: Protect what is yours. Don't go after what is not yours.*

5. *Use what you have and do not be concerned about what you don't have.*

6. *When something is taken away from you, be willing to let it go.*

7. *Put your house in order. Get rid of sorrow, fear, lust, envy, and joy at others' misfortunes) as well as greed, petulance, and over-indulgence.*

All good and evil are based on our choices

"Where lies the good?"

"In our choice."

"Where lies the evil?"

"In our choice."

"And things that are neither good nor evil?"

"Outside our choice."

"So, how many of you remember this outside class? Do you practice this on your own – applying this to your life as readily as you answer questions like, "Is it day?" *Yes.* "Is it night then?" *No.* "Are the stars even in number?" *I can't say.*"

What about money? Are you trained to give the right response "It is not a good"? Have you trained yourself to give right responses or are you simply practicing clever responses? Why should it come as a surprise to you that, in fields you practice, you excel yourself? Or, that you get nowhere in fields you don't?

Understand the nature of praise and blame

A public speaker is confident that he has written a good speech, memorized it, in addition to having a pleasing voice. Why is he still anxious? Because he is not content with being a good speaker, he wants the approval of the audience. He may be well trained in public speaking, but he has no training in dealing with approval and disapproval by others. When did anyone ever tell him about the nature of praise and blame? Or, what kind of praise he should go after and what kind of blame he should avoid? Did he ever receive training in *these* things? Why are you then surprised that he is good at public speaking for which he received training? Or that he is like everyone else in understanding praise and blame for which he has received no training?

He is like a musician who knows how to play an instrument, sing well, dress elegantly and yet feels nervous as he comes on stage. He may know music, but he does know what an audience is, what its applause or mockery amounts to. Nor does he understand his own anxiety: Is he responsible for it? Is someone else responsible? Can it be managed or not? As a result, if he wins a standing ovation, he returns home full of pride; but if he is booed, his bubble is burst, and he is deflated.

Use the gifts you are given to solve all your problems

We experience something similar as well. What do we value? Externals. What are we serious about? Externals. Naturally, we are going to experience fear and anxiety. What else do you expect when you judge an external thing as "bad?" We cannot but be fearful and anxious.

"Please God, let my anxiety go away!"

"Listen, idiot, don't you have the hands that God gave you? Don't complain that your nose is running. Use the hands God gave you to wipe your nose."

Hasn't he given anything that's of help to you here? Has he not given you endurance, nobility, and courage?

When you have "hands" like these, do you still expect someone to wipe your nose? We don't pay attention to such things and we don't care. Show me a single person who cares *how* they do what they do – one who is interested more in the way they behave than in results. Who is concerned with their own action, even while walking around? Who is more concerned about one's plan itself than about the result? If the plan works, the person gets excited and says, "Wow, how well we planned! With a plan like ours, how could we possibly fail?" But if the plan fails, the person is devastated and has nothing more to say on what happened.

None of us consults a seer or spends time praying to understand how one should act. If you know a single person like that, show them to me! I have been looking for a long time for such a noble and gifted person. I don't care if they are young or old, show them to me!

You have been spending all your attention on material things. Then why are you surprised that you end up behaving in a way that is mean, shameful, worthless, cowardly, and weak – a total failure? We don't seem to be concerned about these things and we don't care to practice.

It is your judgements that scare you

Instead of being afraid of death and deportation, if we feared fear itself we would practice avoiding things that we believe are bad. As it stands, we are spirited, fluent, and ready to answer classroom questions and draw the

STOIC CHOICES • 89

right conclusion. In real life though, we are miserably lost at sea. Let a disturbing thought arise, then we will see what we really practiced and trained for. Because we don't practice, we keep piling up worries, believing that our problems are worse than they are.

For example, when I am on a cruise I look around and see nothing but water. I am gripped by fear. What if I drown? I must drink all this sea! It doesn't occur to me that swallowing just three pints of water will do me in. Is it the sea that scares me? No, it is my own judgment that scares me. Or, consider the earthquake. I imagine that the whole city is going to fall on me, even though a little brick will knock my brain out.

"So, what weighs us down and scares us?"

"Our own judgments, obviously"

"What scares you when you are about to leave your country – leaving friends, family, familiar places, and familiar people?"

"Again, our own judgements."

"Children cry when the nanny leaves. Give them a cake and the nanny is forgotten."

"Are you asking us to model ourselves after children?"

"Of course not. You don't need a cake, but correct judgments."

"What are they?"

Practice this all day long

All day long, you should avoid attachment to externals. Not to your friends or to places or to gyms. Not even to your own body. Remember to keep this divine law and always keep it in sight:

- Protect what is yours; don't claim what is someone else's;
- Use what is given to you. Do not desire what not is given to you; and
- When something is taken away from you, give it up readily. Be thankful for the time you had with it. Do not cry like a baby for its mother or nanny.

All slavery is equal

What does it matter what enslaves you and what you are dependent on? How are you any better than someone pining over a girl when you ache for your familiar places, familiar clubs, and diversions like that? Someone comes along and complains he can't drink water from the fountain. What is wrong with regular water?

"But I am used to the fountain water."

"Well, over time, you'll get used to regular water too. And when you get used to this, you will complain if it is taken away from you. You may poetically describe your misery like the line in Euripides: "The baths of Nero, the water of Marcia!" See how tragedy develops when a foolish person faces life's challenges."

"Will I ever see my native city and the city I grew up in?"

"You poor man. Aren't you happy with where you are? What can you see anywhere that is better than the sun, the moon, the stars, the land, and the sea? If you understand that the god you carry within you governs everything, why would you go looking for marble and fine stones? What will you do when it is time for you leave the sun and moon behind? Will you sit down and cry like a baby?"

What did you do in your school? What did you hear? What did you learn? Why do you call yourself a philosopher when all you did was learn a few elementary things and bit of Chrysippus? You hardly crossed the threshold of philosophy. How can you compare yourself to Socrates, who lived and died the way he did? Or with Diogenes, for that matter? Can you imagine them reduced to tears because they weren't going to see this man or that woman? Or that they were no longer in one city but in another? If he can quit a party at a time of his choosing, such a person is not going to sit here feeling sorry for himself. He will stay only if it is fun, like a child involved in playing a game. Such a man would endure deportation whether it is permanent deportation or even death.

"Why aren't you willing to be weaned, as children are, and start eating solid food? Will you never stop crying after your mother and your nanny?"

"By going away, I will make them unhappy."

"*You* will make them unhappy? No. They will be unhappy because of *their* judgments. Get rid of your judgments. If they are smart, they would get rid of their judgments. If they don't they create their own unhappiness."

Be free

As the saying goes, "Man, do something desperate to achieve freedom and tranquility." Lift your head up, like someone released from slavery. Dare to face God and say, "Use me as you like from now on. I am yours and of one mind with you. I refuse nothing that you judge to be good. Lead me where you will. Clothe me in any dress. If it is your will, I will hold any position: officer or citizen, rich or poor, stay here or be banished. No matter what, I will defend you before others. I will show the true nature of things, as they really are."

That's not what you do, is it? You sit indoors waiting for your mother to come and feed you. Imagine what would have happened if [the divine hero in Greek mythology] Heracles had simply hung around the house. He would have been [the cowardly king] Eurystheus, not Heracles. Think about the many friends and companions Heracles made, because he travelled the world. None was closer to him than God and so he was believed to be the son of God. In obedience to God, he went around rooting out crime and injustice. You are no Heracles, you cannot root out the crimes and injustice of others. You are not even [the ancient king] Theseus, otherwise you would have relieved the evils of Attica.

Put your house in order

Then the least you can do is to get your house in order. Instead of getting rid of robbers, get rid of sorrow, fear, lust, envy, and *schadenfreude* (joy at others' misfortunes), greed, petulance, and over-indulgence. But to do this, you need to look up to God and God only and follow His guidance. If you are unwilling to do this, you will end up in sighs and tears. You will be forced to serve someone physically stronger than you. You will seek happiness outside yourself and will never find it. It is because you will be looking for happiness in a place where it is not rather than in a place where it really is.

Think about this

It is crisis time. Make a last desperate effort to gain freedom and tranquility. Discourses II.16.41. Epictetus [RD]

Knowledge is Worthless without Practice

Key ideas of this discourse

1. *You should come to learn philosophy with no conceit.*
2. *We all understand intuitively concepts like good and bad. But we don't know how to apply them properly to a given situation. Therefore, we get into conflict with other.*
3. *It is not enough if you understand these things intellectually and talk about them. You must practice them diligently if you want to make any progress.*

When you want to learn, come without conceit

What is the first order of business when you start learning philosophy? To set aside your self-satisfaction about what you think you know. You are not going to learn anything new, if you think you know it already.

When we come to philosophy we freely talk about what should or should not be done, what is good or bad, what is mean or noble. On that basis, we assign praise or blame, accuse, or condemn, and pass judgments on good and bad behavior, and distinguish one from the other.

We intuitively understand concepts, but not how to apply them properly

Then what do we come to philosophers for? To learn what we think we do not know – the basic principles. Some of us want to learn from philosophers because we think they will be witty and sharp. Others do so because they think they will gain some advantage from it. It is ridiculous to imagine you are going to learn anything other than what you want to learn. You cannot hope to make any progress in any area without putting in the effort. Yet many people make the mistake that [the Greek orator] Theopompous made when he criticized Plato because he wanted to define every word:

[Theopompous] "Did no one before you use the words 'good' and 'just'? If they did, were they just making noise without understanding the meaning of these words?"

[Plato] "Who told you, Theopompous, that we don't intuitively know the meaning of these words? What we don't know is how to apply them correctly. It is impossible to apply these intuitive concepts to life without first understanding to which class of things we can apply each concept. It is like telling physicians, 'Have you not used the terms "sickness" and "health" before Hippocrates came along? Were you then talking nonsense?' Of course, they had an idea of what health was but couldn't agree on how to apply it correctly. One doctor would say, 'Fast' and another would say 'Eat.' One would say, 'Cut a vein' and another would say, 'Give him blood.' Why? Because they could not apply the concept of health correctly to specific instances."

It is so in life as well. We all talk about good and evil, useful, and harmful. It's all in our vocabulary.

"But do we understand how to apply them correctly? Let's see. Prove it."

"How can I prove it?"

Apply them to specific cases. What Plato classifies as "useful," you may classify as "useless." Both of you cannot be right. For some rich is "good," for others it is not. For some, pleasure is "good" and for others health is "good." If all of us understand these intuitive concepts correctly, and need no further clarification, then why do we disagree with one another? Why do we blame one another? But I don't even need to refer to such conflicts. Just look at yourself. If you are good at applying your intuitive concepts properly, why are you unhappy and obstructed?

For now, let's ignore the secondary field of study – impulses and how to regulate them. Let's ignore the third field of study as well – assent. Let's simply look at the first. That alone provides enough proof that you are good at applying intuitive concepts. Are you realistic in your desires, that is, realistic for you? If so, why are you frustrated and unhappy? Aren't you trying to escape the inevitable? How else can you explain your facing misfortunes of any kind? Why do you get what you don't want but not what you do want? This is the greatest proof of misfortune: You want something to happen and it doesn't; you don't want something to happen and it does. Who can be more unfortunate than you?

Tragedy happens when intuitive concepts are misapplied

Isn't this what drove Medea (in Euripides' play) to kill her own children? It was noble in the sense that she realized what it means to have one's desire frustrated. She wanted to take revenge on the man who hurt and humiliated her. How? By killing her children. That would punish her as well, but she didn't care. Thus, a noble soul was ruined. She didn't know where the power lies to do as we wish. We cannot get this power from outside or by rearranging circumstances. If she had given up wanting to keep her husband, she would not have failed to fulfil her desire. If she had given up wanting to live with her husband at any cost, wanting to live in Corinth, and wanting anything but what happens, who would have stopped her or compelled her? No one. She would have been as unstoppable as God himself. When you have God to guide you and conform your wishes to what happens, how can you have any fear of failure?

Make it so that whatever happens is what you want to happen

You may desire wealth and be averse to poverty, but you may end up getting poverty and not wealth. The same is true of the other external things that are outside your choice: health, status, honor, country, friends, or children. Think of these things as God's business and hand them over to him and let him administer them. Make it so that whatever happens is what you want to happen. How can you then be unhappy?

But how can you call yourself educated, if you still experience envy, pity, jealousy, and fear and complain everyday about your condition and about God? What kind of education is that? You learned logic and about changing arguments? Now let go of your past learning and make a fresh start. Realize that you have barely touched upon the most important thing. Begin with this foundation and build on it: Establish how only what you wish to happen happens; nothing you don't wish does.

The three disciplines

Give me a young student who comes to the school with this single purpose, like an athlete in action: "I don't care about the rest. All I want is to spend my life free of obstruction and distress, hold up my head high no matter what happens, and be a free person, a friend of God, fearing nothing that can happen." If any of you can show me that you are such a person, I would say, "Come in, young man, to claim what is your own. You are a credit to philosophy. Yours are all these possessions, books, and discourses.

Thus, when the student learns and masters the first area of study, comes back to me, and says, "I want to be free from fear and emotions. Not just that. As a respectful, philosophical, careful, and attentive person, I would like to know my duty to God, to my parents, siblings, country, and to strangers," I would ask the student to progress to this second area of study.

When the student has mastered the second area of study as well and says, "I have mastered this second area. Now I would like to be secure and unshakable, not just when I am awake but even when I am asleep, drunk, or depressed." My response would be, "You are God. Your goals are praiseworthy!"

Learning means nothing if you don't put it into practice

But no, what do I get? You come and tell me, "I want to master Chrysippus' work on *Liar*.

If that's your plan, you might as well go and jump in the lake. What good will come of it? You will continue to be unhappy while reading it and be anxious when discussing it with others. This is how you talk:

"Shall I read it to you, or you to me?"

"I admire the way you write."

"You write well, in the style of Xenophon."

"You write well too, in the style of Plato."

"You, in the style of Antisthenes."

After having shared your dreams with each other, you go back to your former habits. Your desires and aversions, impulses, designs, and plans don't change. You pray and desire for the same things. You don't look for someone to steer you in the right direction but are offended by any advice. You say, "A mean old man. He didn't feel concerned enough to say 'It's a difficult journey you are going on. I will light a lamp if you return safely.'"

Is that what a good-natured person would have said? Sure, wouldn't it be wonderful for someone like you to come off safe? Isn't it worth lighting lamps for? There is no doubt that someone like you deserves to be free from death and disease!

Throw away this conceit that you possess any useful knowledge. Approach philosophy like you would music or mathematics. Otherwise you won't even come close to making any progress, even if you mastered the complete works of [philosophers like] Chrysippus, Antipater, and Archedemus.

Think about this

Why is it that when you want something, it doesn't come about, and when you don't want it, it comes about? For that's very strong proof that you are in a troubled and unfortunate state. Discourses II.17.17-18. Epictetus [RH]

Choose Habits
That Fight Impressions

Key ideas of this discourse

1. *When you repeat a behavior, it leads to a habit. When you don't repeat a behavior, it does not lead to a habit.*

2. *We sustain habits by feeding behaviors associated with them. When we keep feeding anger, for example, we become ill-tempered.*

3. *We can avoid being carried away by negative passions by not doing the behaviors associated with them.*

4. *Our behaviors are the result of impressions. Don't be carried away by emotions. When an impression creates a negative emotion, take a few minutes to examine its true nature.*

5. *Avoid behaviors that feed a negative habit from the beginning. If you keep postponing, you will reach a stage where you will become too weak to fight them and you will start making excuses.*

When we feed habits, they become strong

Every habit is formed, and every capacity strengthened, by our doing things associated with it. Walking makes you walk better, running makes you run better. Want to be a reader? Read. Want to be a writer? Write. Go for a month without reading, you will see the effect. Lie down for ten days and then try to get up and walk, you'll see how weak your legs have become. So, if you want to do something, make it a habit. If you don't want to do something, do something else in its place.

Each time you are angry you feed the anger habit

This is true of things of the mind as well. When you are angry, it is not an isolated bad thing. You have encouraged a habit, adding fuel to the fire. When you yield to lust, don't think of it as a temporary setback. You have fed and strengthened your weakness. You can expect habits to get stronger by actions associated with them. This is how current habits become stronger and newer habits are formed.

Feeding undesirable habits leads to mental weakness

Here is how you become mentally weak, according to philosophers. When you become greedy, if you use reason to alert you to the danger, your passion will subside, and your mind will be returned to its former balance. But if you don't do anything, the mind will not return to its balanced state, but will be excited by another impression, yielding to passion even more quickly. If you keep yielding to passion, the mind will become insensitive to greed. Eventually, greed will become entrenched.

If you had fever and recovered, you are not in the same state as before, unless you are fully cured. This is true of the unhealthy passions of the mind as well. They leave certain scars and traces behind. Unless you make sure that you are totally cured, the spots that are not fully cured become vulnerable if you have a relapse.

If you don't want a bad habit, don't feed it

So, if you don't want to be bad-tempered, don't feed the habit. Don't do anything that will strengthen the anger habit. Calm down. Don't be angry today. Or the following day. Count the number of days you can go without getting angry. "I used to be angry every day. Then every other day. Then every third," and so on. If you manage to spend thirty days without getting angry, give thanks to God. Your habit was weakened at first and then destroyed. If you continue like this for three or four months without your passion causing you distress as it did before, believe me, you are in excellent health.

Today if I see an attractive person, do not say to yourself, "It would be nice to sleep with this person! How lucky is this person's spouse!" Saying things like that is like saying that an adulterer would be lucky too. I don't start picturing the person taking their clothes off and joining me in bed. Then I congratulate myself and say "Well done, Epictetus. You solved an exceedingly difficult problem, one that's even more difficult than the 'Master' argument." (explained in Discourses II.19.) If the other person is willing, she calls to me, leads me by the arm and snuggles up to me. That would be a hard test. That test would be even harder than *The Liar Paradox* and *The Quiescent*.

[*The Liar Paradox*: If a person says, "I am lying," does she lie or tell the truth? If she lies, then she's telling the truth. If she's telling the truth, then she's lying. Chrysippus is supposed to have written six books on this subject. *The Quiescent*: When do grains make a heap? Two grains? Three? Four? ... A wise person would stop answering such a question.]

How do we resolve it, then? Begin by wanting to please yourself and appear worthy in the presence of God. Desire to become pure in your own eyes and those of God. Then, if you face a dangerous impression, follow Plato's advice. Go to places of worship and atone with sacrifice, so terrible things can be avoided. It is enough even if you seek the company of people of good character. Model your behavior after such people, whether they are alive or dead. Consider Socrates. He lay next to [the Athenian aristocrat] Alcibiades and teased him about his beauty. Think how proud he must have felt to have won a victory over himself. For sure, an Olympic sized victory, worthy of [the founder of Olympic games]

Heracles. We can justly greet that man, rather than boxers, gladiators, and other athletes, "Greetings, hero!"

Don't accept impressions without testing them

If you think of such thoughts when faced with any impression, you will master it and not be swept away by it. Don't get carried away by an impression, no matter how intense it is. Instead, say, "Hey impression, wait for me a while. Let me see what you are and what you represent. Let me test you before accepting you."

Do not let the impression pull you into imagining pleasant consequences of following it. Otherwise it will lead you to any place it wants. Think of a better and more honorable thought to replace the mean and unwholesome impression. Make it a habit. You will see what shoulders, what muscles, and what vigor you develop. As it is, all people do is have academic quibbles. Nothing more. A true trainee is one who trains himself to test any impression that comes his way. Steady yourself, pitiful thing, don't get carried away by impressions. It is a great battle and it is divine. It is a battle to win your kingdom, freedom, happiness, and serenity. Remember God and ask for his help and protection like sailors do in a storm.

Impressions can drive out reason

Is there any storm that is more powerful than impressions that drive out reason? What is a storm itself, except another impression? If you take away the fear of death, all you face is lightning and thunder while the mind remains calm and peaceful. But if you don't do it this time, and say to yourself that you will do it the next time, and then do the same thing the time after that, you can be sure that this is what you will face in the end: You will become so sad and weak that you won't even know where you have gone wrong. You will start making excuses for your behavior confirming (the poet) Hesiod's verse

"Make a bad beginning and you'll contend with troubles ever after."

Think about this

Every habit and faculty is confirmed and strengthened by the corresponding actions, that of walking by walking, that of running by running. Discourses II.18.1. Epictetus [WO]
Make a bad beginning and you'll contend with troubles ever after. Discourses II.18.32. Epictetus [RD]

Choose to Practice, Not to Argue Cleverly

Key ideas of this discourse

- *There are clever arguments like the Master Argument. But they don't contribute to living your life better.*
- *Most people are good at remembering and repeating what the great philosophers said. That's of no use either unless we judge for ourselves the truth about the impressions we encounter.*
- *We are good at explaining how we should deal with impressions. But faced with a real-life crisis, we are unable to apply what we learned. Talking the talk is not enough. We need to walk the walk.*
- *So far, we have not succeeded in walking the walk. Whether it is my fault, your fault, or the fault of both us, let's leave the past behind. Let's make a fresh start.*

The Master Argument

The 'Master' argument goes something like this: There are three propositions but all three cannot be true at the same time.

1. Everything true as an event in the past is necessarily true.
2. An impossibility cannot be the consequence of a possibility.
3. Something that is not true, and never will be true, is possible.

[The Greek historian] Diodorus realized that these arguments were inconsistent. He accepted the first two propositions to be true, but not the third. He was followed by someone else who rejected the first proposition but accepted the other two to be true. [Stoic philosophers] Cleanthes and Antipater seemed to have accepted the latter view. There are others who believe the first and third, that something is possible that is not, and never will be, true, and that everything that has happened is necessarily true, but the impossible may be a consequence of the possible. However, we cannot retain all three as true because they are mutually incompatible.

The Master Argument is of little practical use

If anyone should ask me, "What do you think?" I would reply, "I don't know. All I can report is what opinions Diodorus, Panthoides, Cleanthes, or Chrysippus held."

"But what about you?"

"It is none of my business. I wasn't born to test my impressions against what people say so I can form my own opinion on the subject. If I did that I wouldn't be any different from a student of literature."

[This dialog indicates that Epictetus takes a dim view of arguments for arguments' sake that propositions like these seem to generate, as the dialog below confirms.]

"Who was Hector's father?"

"Priam."

"His brothers?"

"Alexander and Deiphobus."

"Their mother?"

"Hecuba. So I've heard."

"Where?"

"In Homer. And Hellenicus too. Perhaps one or two other writers who specialize in these matters."

Don't keep repeating what other have said

And that's how I feel about the Master argument. What can I add to what has been said already? If I am vain and want to astonish people, especially at a party, I can catalogue who said what:

- Chrysippus has written so well on the subject in the first chapter of his book *On Possibles*.

- Cleanthes and Archedemus have devoted an entire book to the topic.

- Then there is Antipater who contributed to *On Possibles* and wrote a separate monograph on the Master Argument.

"Haven't you read it?"

"No, I haven't."

"Do read it, then."

What good will it do him? He will find it harder to shut up than he does already. And what did you gain by reading it? What opinions did you form? Sure, you will tell us all about Helen and Priam and the Calypso island, none of which ever existed or ever will. In literary matters, it doesn't matter much if you remember the story and don't form your own judgment about it. But it is unfortunate when we do so in matters of conduct.

"Tell me. What is good and bad?"

"Listen. The wind has blown me from a far-off place to here. Anything can be good, bad, or indifferent. Virtues, and anything that shares in them, are good. Vices, and anything that shares in them, are bad. Everything in between, such as wealth, health, life or death, pleasure or pain, is indifferent."

"How do you know this?"

"I read it in a book *Egyptian History* by Hellanicus."

"How is it different from saying that you read it by some other author such as Chrysippus or Cleanthes? In some other book such as *Ethics*? Have you tested these principles yourself and formed your own judgment?"

Show me how you apply what you learned

Tell me how you would behave when you meet with a storm on board a ship, as the sails flap madly in the wind. Would you still remember these distinctions among good, bad, and indifferent? What if someone teases you saying, "Remind me, what were you just saying about good, bad, and indifferent? Is getting caught in a shipwreck good, bad, or indifferent?" Aren't you likely to hit the man with a piece of wood and say, "Why are you torturing me? We are about to drown, and you think this is funny?"

When an emperor sends for you to answer a charge, would you remember the distinctions you talked about? When you go to face charges, pale and shaking, what if someone came up to you and said, "Why are you shaking, my friend? What are you afraid of? The emperor cannot make things good or bad for you."

"Why do you make fun and add to my troubles?"

"Tell me anyway, philosopher. Why are you shaking? All you are facing is death, prison, torture, exile, or disgrace. Are any of these things a vice or connected with a vice? Remind me, what were you used to calling these things?"

"Why do you bug me? I have enough evils to contend with."

You said it well here. Your own evils – your meanness, cowardice, and pretension – are enough for you. Why do you brag about things that are not your own? Why even call yourself a Stoic?

Just observe the way you behave, and you will soon discover what your philosophy is. Most of you will find that you are Epicureans, some are Peripatetics [followers of Aristotle] and even that without backbones. By what action can you prove that virtue is equal, if not superior, to everything else?

We all talk the talk.
One who walks the walk is hard to find

Show me a stoic if you can find one. You can indeed show me a thousand people who can repeat petty stoic arguments. They can talk the talk. They can talk equally well about Epicurean principles. Or about the Peripatetic principles.

Who then is a Stoic? We call a statue "Pheidian," if it is made in the style of Pheidias. So, show me someone who shapes himself according his beliefs. Show me someone who is sick and yet happy; in danger and yet happy; dying and yet happy; condemned to exile and yet happy; lost his reputation and yet happy. Show him to me, by god, I long to see a Stoic!

You may say that you don't know anyone so perfectly formed. All right. Then show me someone who is on the way to becoming one, someone walking in the right direction. Do me a favor. Don't refuse this old man a sight he has never seen. And don't show me the golden and ivory idols of Zeus, Pheidias, or his Athena. Show me a living person with a soul that never criticizes god or fellow human beings ever again, whose wishes never fail to come true, who never falls into anything he wants to avoid, who is never angry, envious, or jealous, and who desires to be godlike instead of just being human. A person, though in this lifeless body, is in communion with God. Show him to me. You cannot, can you? So why kid yourself and delude others? Why assume an identity that doesn't belong to you? You are like thieves who take clothes and property that don't belong to them.

Manage your impressions if you want to be free

Here I am, your teacher. You have come here to be instructed by me. It is my ambition to secure you from restraint, compulsion, and obstruction, and to make you free, prosperous, and happy, with your attention fixed on God in everything big or small. You are here to learn and practice these things. Why don't you do it then, if you have the right resolve and I the proper qualifications? What is missing? When I see an artisan at work with the right material, I expect to see a finished product. Now here is an artisan and here is the material. What's missing? Can this thing not be taught? No, it can be taught. Is it outside our power? No, this is the only thing that is within our power. Not wealth, health, or fame. Nothing is in our power except the power to use impressions correctly. By nature, this alone cannot be restrained and hindered.

Tell me, then, why you fail to succeed? Either it is your fault or mine. Or the fault lies in the task. But the task is manageable and is totally in our power. It follows then that the fault lies with you or me or, more likely, with both of us.

Well then, are you prepared, at last, to begin the task with me? Set the past aside. Just begin. Trust me, you will see what I have been saying is true.

Think about this

I have this purpose: To make you free from restraint, compulsion, hindrance, to make you free, prosperous, and happy...and you are here to learn and practice these things. Discourses II.19.29. Epictetus [GL]

Choose the Right Doctrine to Guide You

Key ideas of this discourse

1. *Some ideas are so true that even those who deny the truth of such ideas are forced to make use of them.*
2. *For example, Epicurus says that people don't have natural goodwill towards one another. But the fact that he spends time correcting others shows that he cares whether others are misled by wrong opinions or not. This demonstrates that he has goodwill toward others.*
3. *Illogical doctrines can be harmful. We should use our rational faculty and evaluate impressions the right way.*

The illogical doctrine of Epicurus

Some statements are true and obvious. Even those who contradict them are obliged to accept them. It is about the strongest proof one could offer that a statement is true when those who contradict it make use of it.

Suppose a person denies that some statements are universally true. Then he has to say, "There is no statement that is universally true." Then this statement cannot be true either. It is like saying that if a statement is universal, it is false. How about this? Someone tells you,

"Know this. We can know nothing for sure. Everything is uncertain." Or,

"Trust me and you'll be glad you did. You can't trust anyone," Or,

"It is impossible to learn anything. I will teach you why this is so."

What is the difference between these people and those who call themselves "Academics" who say, "Agree to the statement that 'no one ever agrees to a statement.'" Or, "Trust us when we say that no one trusts anyone."

Epicurus is no different. In trying to demonstrate that human beings don't have natural goodwill for one another, he demonstrates that they do. What does he say?

"Don't be deceived, misled or mistaken, you fools. Rational beings have no goodwill toward one another. Trust me. People who say otherwise are deceiving you and leading you astray with false reasoning."

"Why should *you* care then? Let's be led astray."

By refuting the truth, Epicurus proves it

[The following is directed at Epicurus.] You will not be any worse off if all of us are convinced that natural good will exists among human beings and we need to preserve it. Wouldn't we be much better off and more secure? Why then, my friend, do you concern yourself with us, stay awake, light your lamp, rise early, and draft such big books? Is it because you are worried that some of us may be misled into believing that God cares for us? Or we may come to believe that the essence of goodness can be something other than pleasure?

In that case, drop everything and go to sleep. Live like a worm that you have judged human beings to be. Eat, drink, have sex, move your bowels, and snore. What is it to you what we think about these things? Why should you care if our views are correct or not? What do we have to do with you?

Do you worry about sheep because they are available to you to be shorn, milked, and slaughtered? Would you like it if human beings, lulled and sedated by Stoic teachings, are similarly available for your use? You should have reserved your teachings for your fellow-Epicureans, away from other human beings. Instead, you should persuade us that we are born with a sense of natural fellowship and virtue is a good thing, so everything can be to your advantage. Or do we offer our fellowship only to some people and not to others? If so, to whom? To those who would offer us their fellowship back or those who would not?

No one violates the idea of fellowship more than Epicureans who have set up such doctrines. So, what made Epicurus get out of bed and write these things? It is nature. Nature is enormously powerful and strong and makes people do things for its own purpose, even when people are unwilling. Nature says,

"Since you hold these unsocial opinions, stay awake and write them down. Pass them on to others. Let your own behavior disprove your writings."

[In Greek mythology] we read about the Furies hounding Orestes and waking him from his sleep. It is worse for Epicurus. The Furies and the avenging spirits wake him from his sleep and would not even let him rest. They force him to make his miserable views public, like wine and madness do the priest of Cybele. Nature is that irresistible.

Human beings don't lose their affections

A vine cannot behave like an olive tree or an olive tree like a vine. It is impossible. Neither can human beings lose their affections. A man cannot get rid of his sexual desires by cutting off his male organs. So, it is with Epicurus. He cut off all that defines a human being: being the head of a family, a citizen, and a friend. But he could not cut off his human desires any more than the lazy Academics could set aside their sense-perceptions, even though they tried hard. It is a pity. After all, nature has given us rules by which anyone can discover the truth. Instead of trying to improve them and make up for their shortcomings, they do precisely the opposite. They try to take away and destroy everything that could help them to discover the truth.

"Tell me, philosopher, what do you think of piety and sanctity?"

"I can prove they are good things, if you like."

"Do prove it so our citizens may look up to and honor the divine and no longer neglect things of greatest importance."

"Do you have the proofs, then?"

"I do, indeed. And I am thankful."

"Since you are so pleased with your proofs, listen to these challenges [patterned after the Academics]. God doesn't exist. If he does, he does not care for humans and we have nothing in common with him. The piety and sanctity you talk about is just a lie told by swindlers and crooks or, if you believe it, by lawmakers to frighten and deter the criminals from breaking the law."

Well done, philosopher. Our citizens are so much better for you. You have rescued young people who were already developing contempt for the divine.

"What? You aren't pleased? Then listen to this. Justice is nothing, reverence is stupidity, being a father means nothing and being a son is nothing."

Well said, philosopher. Keep it up, convince young people so they think and talk like you. It is these principles that made well-governed cities great. Cities like Sparta owes its very existence to such principles. Through his laws and educational programs, [the legendary lawgiver] Lycurgus instilled the following value such as this into Spartans: it is no more shameful to be a servant than it is to be a powerful person. People who died in the battles such as of Thermopylae died for such principles. Principles like this also motivated Athenians to abandon their city.

Then there are those who talk in this way yet get married, produce children, engage in public affairs, and become priests or prophets. Of whom? Of God, who does not exist? They consult other priests in turn, only to be told lies in the form of false oracles. What shameless cheats!

What are you doing? You contradict yourself every day and yet won't give up your useless efforts. When you eat, where do you bring your hand? To your mouth or to your eye? Where do you go when you want to bathe? Do you ever call a pot a dish? Or a spoon a skewer? If I worked for a philosopher like that, I would goad him constantly, even if was punished. If he asked me to prepare his bath with oil, I would pour some fish sauce over his head. If he said,

"What is the meaning of this?"

"You are in luck. I received the impression that bath oil and fish sauce are indistinguishable."

If he asked me to bring him soup, I would bring vinegar.

"Did I not ask for the soup?"

"Yes, this is the soup."

"Isn't this vinegar?"

"Is vinegar any different from soup?"

"Here, smell and taste it."

"How do you know that our senses don't deceive us?"

If there were three or four like-minded fellow servants, I would make him go mad or hang himself. Or change his opinions!

Illogical principles can have harmful effects

But, as it stands, it is they who are making fun of us. They enjoy all the resources that nature provides as they talk about abolishing them. Grateful and modest people indeed! They eat bread every day and yet pretend that they don't know whether God exists. They enjoy night and day, the changing seasons, the stars, the earth, the sea, and the help they receive from others, but they pay no attention to all these. They state their argument, clear their stomachs, and go off to have a bath. They have given no thought to what they will say, about what, and to whom. They have not given any thought to its significance, such as how a promising young person might be so affected by such talk that he may be persuaded not to realize his potential. Such principles can provide rationale for adultery, justification for stealing, and motivation for rebelling against one's parents.

But there's no point trying to convince such insensitive philosophers

What is good and evil, noble, or mean – this or that? Why bother challenging these philosophers? Why argue with them or try to change their mind? You will have a better chance of changing someone's sexual orientation than trying to change these philosophers who have become deaf and blind.

Think about this

Oh, what a misfortune it is that when man has received from nature measures and standards for discovering the truth, he doesn't go on to try to add to them and make up for what is missing, but does precisely the opposite, and if he possesses some capacity that would enable him to discover the truth, he tries to root it out and destroy it. Discourses II.20.21. Epictetus [RH]

DISCOURSE 21

Guard Against Your Inconsistencies

Key ideas of this discourse

1. *We admit to some of our faults but not to others.*
2. *When we see a fault as something beyond our control, we admit to it. When we see it as something that should be under our control, we don't admit to it.*
3. *But we are confused about what is under our control and what is not under our control.*
4. *Many students start studying philosophy not to live it, but to impress others with their knowledge. So, their life continues to be the same as before.*
5. *For these principles to work, you should approach them with a clear mind and put them into practice.*

We admit only to some of our faults

We readily admit to some of our faults, but not to others. For example, we wouldn't admit to being foolish or stupid, but say things like, "I wish I had as much luck as I have sense," or, "Maybe I'm a bit timid, but I am no fool." Hardly anyone would admit to a lack of self-control, to being unjust, or to being nosy or envious. Most would, however, admit that they are moved by pity.

Why is this?

The main reason is that we are confused and inconsistent about what is good and evil. We may differ from one another but, as a rule, we wouldn't admit to anything that we consider shameful. We may consider timidity and pity as signs of being sensitive, but stupidity as a sign of being slavish. Least of all are we willing to admit to antisocial behavior. We acknowledge those faults we consider involuntary – such as shyness and timidity. A person who lacks self-control may rebrand it as love and expect to be forgiven for this involuntary reaction. But injustice cannot be justified as involuntary. Jealousy is involuntary to a certain extent, so people will admit to it.

We should examine ourselves

We are surrounded by people who are so confused and so ignorant of what they are saying. Whatever fault they may have, wherever they may have got it from, and

however they may get rid of it, we should make it a habit
to ask ourselves the following questions:

- Am I one of them too?
- What conceit do I have?
- Do I conduct myself as a sensible and moderate person?
- Do I say that I am educated enough to face anything that might happen?
- Am I aware that I know nothing, since I know nothing?
- Do I go to my teacher and follow his instructions as if they came from an oracle?
- Or, like others, do I go there like a sniveling child, only to study the history of philosophy, memorize bookish principles and explain them to others?

Quit complaining

You have been fighting with your help at home. Your
household is a mess. You have disturbed your neighbors'
peace. Now you have come here looking all dignified and
scholarly. And you see fit to pass judgement on how I
explain a text and say whatever nonsense that comes to
my head?

You have come here in a spirit of envy because you
get no allowance from home. You sit through my lectures
and discussions while thinking all the while about how
things are between you and your father or brother.
"What are they saying about me back home? I suppose I
am making progress and they are saying, 'He will come

back knowing everything.' At one point, I suppose, I had hoped I would know everything. But that is demanding work and I get no help from home. The baths here are awful. Things are going badly for me both at home and here."

Then people start saying that one is no better off for attending school. Who – I repeat who – goes to school to become a better person? Who goes to have their judgments examined, fully aware that they need to be examined? Is it any wonder you go back home with the same set of ideas that you came here with? You did not come here to have your ideas examined. Not in the least. Far from it. So at least think about this. Are you getting what *you* came here for? You want to chatter about philosophical principles. Well, aren't you getting better at that? Haven't you become more talkative than you were before? Aren't these topics that give you enough material for you to impress others? Haven't you learned logic and how to analyze an argument? Haven't you learned assumptions in *The Liar* and other hypothetical arguments?

"Why then are you unhappy, even though you got everything you came here for?"

"Well, what good will all this do me if my child dies? Or if my brother or myself have to die or suffer torture?"

"Did you come here for that? Did you sit beside me for that? Is it for that you sometimes sacrificed sleep and studied all night? Did you ever, when you went for a walk, challenge an impression in your mind and examine it with your colleagues, rather than arguing about logic? When did you ever do that?"

And then you say the principles you learn here are useless. Useless to whom? Only to those who apply them incorrectly. Eye drops are not useless if applied to eyes the right way. Neither are bandages. Weights are not useless to everyone; they are useful to some and not to others. If you ask me, "Is logic useful?" I would say, "Yes. I will show you how if you like."

"What good has it done me?"

"You didn't ask me whether it was useful to you personally but whether it was useful in general. Vinegar is useful to someone suffering from indigestion."

"So, is it useful to me now?"

"No, not to you now. You need to have the discharge stopped first and have the wounds healed."

All of you, heal your ulcers, stop the discharges, and calm your mind. Bring it to the school, free from distractions. Only then will you know how powerful reason can be.

Think about this

First, cure your ulcers, stop your discharges, be tranquil in mind, bring it free from distraction into the school; then you will know what power reason has. Discourses II.21.22. Epictetus [WO]

Choose to Be a True Friend

Key ideas of this discourse

1. *You cannot love anyone if you cannot tell the difference between what is good, what is bad, and what is indifferent.*

2. *We readily admit to our faults, if we believe we are not truly responsible for them, but not when we believe we are responsible for them.*

3. *But we are mistaken about which ones are truly our faults and which ones are not. We are responsible for our judgments and not for externals.*

4. *We are all driven by self-interest. The way to be a friend it to relate friendship and love to our self-interest rather than to external things. If we expect to gain some external benefit from another person, we cannot love them, and we cannot be their loyal friend.*

The power of love belongs to the wise

You love whatever you are interested in. Is anyone interested in being evil? Is anyone interested in things that do not concern them? Of course not. It follows then that people are interested in good things. If they are interested in them, they love them too. So, if you know what is good, you will also love it. But if you are incapable of distinguishing good, bad, and neutral things, how can you be capable of love? The power of love, then, belongs only to the wise.

"Really? I don't claim to be wise, but I love my child."

"You surprise me. First you admit that you are not wise. What is missing? Your senses work, you can differentiate among impressions, and you eat, clothe, and provide shelter for yourself. Why then do you say you lack wisdom?"

We are often confused by sense impressions

Let me explain it to you. You are often dazed and confused by sense impressions. You are overcome by them. You consider something as good, then you consider the same thing as bad, and still later you decide the very same thing is neither good nor bad. Such indecision results in pain, fear, jealousy, turmoil, and inconsistency. That's why you are not wise, as you readily admit.

Don't you also change your mind about love? What about pleasure, wealth, and other material things? Don't you consider the same things as good or bad at various times? Don't you judge the same person to be good sometimes and bad at other times? Praise them at one moment and reproach them at another?

"Yes, I admit I do."

"Well, can you be someone's friend if you hold wrong impressions about them?"

"Of course not."

"If you are prone to change your mind about a friend, can your feelings toward that friend be warm?"

"No again."

"If you first blame and later admire the same person?"

"No not then either."

"Haven't you thought, 'nothing could be friendlier,' when you saw little dogs playing and fawning on one another? But just throw some meat in the middle and you will know what this friendship is."

We are driven by self-interest

It is the same with us. Put a piece of real estate between you and your son, he would wish that you were dead and buried. And you him. "Some child I raised. He wants me dead!" Place a pretty girl between an older and a younger man, both fall equally hard for the girl. So it is with any kind of honor. If your life is at stake, you will end up saying the same thing Admetus' father said to his son: "You want to see the light, don't you imagine your father does too?" [From Euripides' *Alcestis*, line 691. Robert Dobbin's translation.]

Do you think that he did not love his own child when he was small? Did he not suffer when the child had a fever and say, "If only I could be sick instead"? But, when the time comes to face a choice, just see what he says!

You cannot be a loyal friend if your self-interest is tied to externals

Eteocles and Polyneices shared the same parents and were brought up together. They often kissed each other. Anyone who saw them laughed at philosophers for their paradoxical view on friendship. Yet when time came to decide which one of them would be king, see what they say:

Eteocles: "Where will you stand before the tower?"
Polyneices: "Why do you ask?"
Eteocles: "I mean to face and kill you."
Polyneices: "So do I."

They even pray so their wish can come true. Have no illusions, this is a universal law: Every creature is attached to nothing as strongly as to its own interest. Whatever appears to threaten its interest – be it brother, father, child, or lover – is hated, accused, and cursed. We are naturally disposed to favor our own interest. This is our father, brother, relatives, country, and god. If we believe that God is hindering us, we are ready to turn even on him, smash his statues, and burn his temples. This is what Alexander did when he burned down the temple of Aesculapius because his loved one died.

For this reason, if you believe that your interests are served through piety, honesty, country, parents, and friends, they are safe. But once you believe that your interests are different, all these are lost, outweighed by self-interest. Everyone moves towards what is "me" and "mine." If you believe your interests are served by your body, it will dominate your life; if it is moral choice, then it is moral choice that will dominate; and if external things, then it is external things. You will be where your choices are.

So, you can be a friend, a son, or a father only if it is where you think your interests are. Here you see your interests will be served by being faithful, honest, patient, tolerant, co-operative, and thus maintain your social relations. But, if you separate your self-interest from honor, then the result would be to provide support to the Epicurus doctrine, "Honor doesn't exist. If it does, it is what people agree to."

Valuing externals has led to many tragic outcomes

It is this type of ignorance that made Athenians turn on Spartans, Spartans on Athenians, and Thebans on both; King of Persia to invade Greece, and Macedonians invade both; and, in our times, it led to the battle of Gatea [in which the Roman emperor Trajan fought with the kingdom Dacia]. Going further back, it caused the Trojan war. Paris was Menelaus' guest. Anyone who saw how much goodwill was between them would never have believed they were not friends. Between them was thrown a temptation – a pretty woman. And they went to war.

So, when you see friends or siblings who seem to be of one mind, don't rush to say anything about their friendship. Not even if they swear to it and say it is impossible to separate them. You cannot trust a bad person's judgement. It's weak, unstable, and readily influenced by one impression after another.

Don't simply ask, as others do, "Do they share the same parents?" or, "Did they grow up together?" or, "Did they go to the same school?" Just ask where they put their self-interest – things outside of themselves or in their power to choose? If their self-interest lies in external things, don't call them friends any more than you would call them trustworthy, consistent, determined, or free. No, don't even call them human beings, if you are wise. Because no human judgment can make people snap at others or insult them, take over the marketplace like the wild animals take over the mountains and deserts, or act in courts of justice like gangsters. No human judgment can lead people to be self-indulgent, adulterous, and corrupt or lead to them commit crimes that people commit against each other.

These things are the result of one thing and one thing only. These people place their self-interest in externals, outside their power of choice. But if you hear that they sincerely believe that good lies with what is in their choice and where impressions are used correctly, then don't bother to find out if they belong to the same family or are long-term friends, even if it is the only thing you know about them. You can be confident that they are friends, fair and reliable. Where else can you find friendship if not with fairness, reliability, and respect for what is honorable – and these things only?

"But she has been paying attention to me all this time. Does she not love me?"

"How do you know, stupid, that she hasn't paid attention to you in the way she attends to her shoes when he polishes them or the way she attends to her horse? And how do you know that, once you are no longer of use to her, she would not throw you away like a broken plate?"

"But she is my wife. We have lived together a long time."

"So did Eriphyle. She was with Amphiaraus for a long time and was the mother of his children. Yet a necklace came between them." [Eriphyle was bribed with a necklace to get her husband to join Polynecices against Eteocles in the war to take over Thebes.]

What does this necklace signify? One's judgement about externals like the necklace. This was the animal-like element that destroyed their love. The wife would not remain a wife and the mother would not remain a mother.

The only way to be a good friend

If you are serious about being a friend, get rid of such judgments. Despise them and drive them out of your mind. This way

- You will avoid criticizing yourself. You will be free of inner conflict, an unstable mind and self-torment; and

- You will be in a condition to be a friend to others. You will have a frank and open relationship with like-minded people. With people not like you, you will be patient, gentle, kind, and forgiving. You will keep in mind that they are ignorant or mistaken about what is most important.

You will be harsh with no one, being convinced of the truth of Plato's words,

"Every soul is deprived of the truth against its will."

If you don't follow this, you may do many things that friends normally do – such drinking, living, and traveling together. You may even share the same parents, but so do many snakes. But you can never be friends if you hold these inhuman and despicable judgments.

Think about this

For where else can friendship be found than where fidelity lies, and where a sense of shame lies, and where there is respect for what is right and nothing other than that? Discourses II.22.30. Epictetus [RH]

Choice is Your Best Faculty, Don't Be Distracted

Key ideas of this discourse

This discourse cautions us against neglecting faculties that are less important than choice. Our hearing, sight etc. may not be as important as our ability to choose, but they are valuable. But we should be careful not to get carried away by them and forget to do the most important thing - choose correctly and use impressions according to nature.

1. *All faculties are gifts from God. But not all faculties are of equal value.*

2. *The faculty of choice is the supreme one. It makes use of the other faculties.*

3. *While we should realize that all faculties have their uses, we should not lose sight of the supreme faculty of choice.*

4. *Pursuing lesser faculties at the expense of the supreme faculty is like a traveler forgetting to come home.*

5. *You should use impressions according to nature, not fail in your desires, not experience anything you don't desire, and never face misfortune, but be free, unrestricted, and unrestrained.*

Our senses are witnesses to God's existence

Everyone would read a legibly written book with immense pleasure and ease. Everyone would also listen with great ease to discussions that are expressed in graceful and well-composed prose. So, we must not say that there is no such thing as the faculty of expression. Doing so would make us impious and cowardly. Impious, because we are ignoring the gift from God. It is like denying the usefulness of vision, hearing, or speech.

Did God give you eyes for no reason – giving them such a strong spirit and devising them so cleverly that they can see things at great distances and register the shape of whatever they see? What messenger is that fast and that accurate? Was it for nothing that he made the air between your eyes and the things you see so active and elastic, that vision flows through it? Was it for nothing he made light, without which everything else would be useless?

God has given us something even greater: the faculty of choice

Don't be ungrateful for these gifts. Remember as well that there are even better things. Give thanks to God for sight, hearing, life, and whatever supports life – things such as fruits, wine, and oil. But remember, he has given you something of far greater value than any of these. It is the faculty that uses all these things, judges them, and evaluates their worth. What is this faculty? Is it each faculty itself? You have not heard sight or hearing saying something about itself. These faculties are just servants and subordinates to obey the faculty that can judge impressions.

- If you want to know the value of anything, whom do you ask? Who answers your question? How then can any faculty be superior to this one which uses the services of all other faculties, tests them, and evaluates their worth?

- Which other faculty knows about itself – what it is, how much it is worth, and when it should or should not be used?

- Which faculty opens and closes our eyes, and directs their attention towards some objects and away from others? Sight itself? No. It is the faculty of choice.

- What makes us curious and inquisitive, so we listen to something? And what makes us unmoved, so we don't listen to it? Hearing itself? No. It is the faculty of choice.

The faculty of choice notices that the other faculties are deaf and blind, incapable of looking after anything else except for functions they are designed for. Only the faculty of choice can see clearly enough to evaluate the worth of all other faculties, as well as its own worth, and declare that it is the supreme faculty.

An eye that is open has no choice but to see. But it is the faculty of choice that decides whether you should use it to look at a person's spouse, and how. What faculty tells you as to whether you should believe or disbelieve what someone tells you? If you believe it, should you be angry about it? Is it not the faculty of choice that tells you that?

The faculty of expression and embellishment of language, if it is really a faculty, does nothing more than dress up and rearrange words on a given topic, the way a hairdresser rearranges hair. But whether to speak or to keep quiet; and, if to speak, whether to speak this way or that, whether it is appropriate or not, and the right time and utility for each action – what else decides these things except the faculty of choice? How can you, then, expect it to come forward and talk against itself?

"What then, let us accept that all this is true. Yet it is possible that a subordinate can be superior to the one it serves – such as the horse to the rider, the dog to the hunter, the instrument to the musician, or the servants to the master."

"What uses everything else? Choice. What takes care of everything? Choice. What destroys a person, sometimes by hunger, sometimes by hanging, and sometimes by falling off the cliff? Choice. Is there anything stronger in a human being than this?"

How can something that can be restrained be stronger than something that cannot be? What has the natural

STOIC CHOICES • 143

power to obstruct seeing? Both choice and external things. They can also obstruct speech and hearing. But no external can obstruct choice. Only choice, when corrupted, can obstruct itself. Therefore, choice alone is vice. And choice alone is virtue.

A challenge to Epicurus

Since choice is such a great faculty, and is put in charge of other faculties, let it come forward and say that flesh is the most excellent thing. Even if the flesh called itself most excellent, no one would tolerate it. What made you say such a thing, Epicurus? What made you write *On the End* [a book on ethics] or *The Physics* or *On the Standard* [a book on epistemology]? What made you grow a philosopher's long beard? Which part of you made you say, when you were about to die, that you were spending your last and, at the same time, happiest day? Was this the flesh, or the faculty of choice? Unless you are mad, can you then claim anything is superior to choice? Or are you deaf and blind?

Lesser faculties have their uses

Does this mean we should look down upon the other faculties? Of course not. That would be stupid, impious, and ungrateful towards God. Let's give each thing its due. Even a donkey has some use, though not as much as an ox. A dog has some use, though not as much as a servant. A servant has some use, though not as much as their fellow citizens. Fellow citizens have some use, but not as much as the magistrates. Although some things are of greater value, we should not disregard the contribution of others. The faculty of expression has its value, but it is not as great as the faculty of choice.

Therefore, when I say this, don't any of you assume that I am asking you to be careless about how you express yourself. It wouldn't be any truer than thinking that I would ask you to neglect your eyes, ears, hands, feet, clothes, or shoes. But if you ask me what is the highest of all things, what I am to say? The faculty of eloquence? No, I cannot say that. It is the faculty of choice, when we make the right choice. It is this faculty that controls the faculty of eloquence as well as all other faculties, great and small. If this is set right, a person becomes good; if it goes wrong, a person becomes bad. This is what decides whether one is fortunate or not and whether we would be friendly or hostile toward someone. Simply put, this is what produces unhappiness when neglected and happiness when cared for.

But to do away with the faculty of eloquence and consider it as nothing is being ungrateful toward those who have given it. It is cowardly too. If you believe that the faculty of expression doesn't exist, maybe you are afraid that you wouldn't be able to ignore it if it did. It is like people denying the difference between beauty and ugliness. Could a person be affected the same way by seeing Thersites [who is said to be "bow-legged and lame, to have shoulders that cave inward, and a head which is covered in tufts of hair"] as seeing Achilles? Or at the sight of Helen as at that of any ordinary woman? No, ignorant and crude people, who have no discriminating power, hold such ideas. They are worried that if they see the difference, they will be overcome by it right away and lose control.

This is the important thing: Leave everything to its own faculty and then see what value it has. Then recognize the faculty in charge of them and pursue it with full attention. Make everything else secondary to it, without neglecting even these, to the extent possible. For example, we should take care of our eyes, not because they are of the highest importance, but because they serve the faculty of highest importance. The highest faculty needs the use of eyes, along with reason, to choose one thing over another.

Do not get distracted by lesser faculties

What do people usually do? They behave like a traveler returning home who comes across an inn, finds it comfortable and stays there. Have you forgotten your purpose? You were not traveling to this, but through this.

"But this is a fine inn."

"Sure. There are many other fine inns and many pleasant pastures. They are just way stations. Your business is to return to your country, to relieve the anxieties of your family, and be a citizen; to get married, raise children, and be employed."

You did not come into this world to pick the most charming place to live but to live in the country of your birth or in a country of which you are a citizen. Something similar goes on in the matter of eloquence as well. To advance towards perfection, you need to use spoken words to learn what is taught here, to purify your choice, and to deal correctly with impressions. Because this knowledge must be taught through certain principles and in a certain style, we express it using variety and forceful style. Some people get carried away by such things and want to stay put: some by style, some by logic, some by equivocal arguments, and some by another "inn." And there they remain as if they are among Sirens.

Your business, my friend, is to prepare yourself to use impressions according to nature, not fail in your desires, not experience anything you don't desire, and never face misfortune, but be free, unrestricted, and unrestrained. Conform to God's rule and willingly submit to it. Find fault with no one and accuse no one. Be able to say with sincerity the verse [written by Cleanthes] which begins with, "Lead me, Zeus; Lead me, Destiny."

Although you have this purpose, are you going to choose to stay where you are because some turn of phrase or abstract principles caught your fancy? Are you going to forget your home and say, "It's nice here"? No one is saying it is not, but it is only a way station, an inn. You can be as eloquent as Demosthenes and yet be unhappy. Even if you are as good in logic as Chrysippus, what is to prevent you being uneasy, sad, and envying – in other words, being disturbed and miserable? Nothing. So, you see, these inns are of no value, because you have a different purpose.

When I talk like this, some people assume that I am against rhetoric and other principles of presentation. No, I am not. I am only against people endlessly pursuing them and placing their hopes in them. If anyone thinks that such views cause harm, then consider me the most harmful person. When I see that something is of the highest value and is supreme, I am not going to say it is something else, just to make you happy.

Think about this

Man, your purpose was to make yourself competent to use conformably with nature the external impressions that came to you, in desire not to fail in what you would attain, and in avoidance not to fall into what you would avoid, never suffering misfortune... Discourses II.23.42 Epictetus [WO]

Show Yourself to Be Worthy

Key ideas of this discourse

1. *If you want someone of knowledge to talk to you, you should first arouse enthusiasm in that person to talk to you.*
2. *To excite a philosopher to talk to you, you should first demonstrate that you are capable of learning.*

Speaking well involves skill and so does listening

Someone said to Epictetus:

"I have come to you many times, wanting to listen to you. But you have never given me an answer. But now, if possible, please say something to me."

"Do you think that there is an art to speaking with skill? If you don't possess this skill you will speak unskillfully?"

"I believe so, yes."

"Someone whose speech benefits oneself and others would be speaking with skill, and someone whose speech harms oneself and others would be speaking unskillfully. You would find that some suffer harm and others gain benefit. Do all listeners gain benefit from what they hear, or some gain benefit while others suffer harm?"

"Not all would gain benefit."

"Skillful listeners benefit, and unskillful listeners are harmed?"

"Yes."

"Just as there is a skill in speaking, there is a skill in listening?"

"It would seem so."

"Consider it from another point of view, if you please. Whose job it is to play a musical instrument according to the rules of music?"

"The musician's."

"All right. Whose job is it to make a statue properly?"

"The sculptor's."

"Don't you think that it requires skill also to appreciate the statue properly?"

"Yes, it does."

Don't you see then, if speaking properly demands a skilled person, to listen with benefit also demands a skilled person? For the time being, let's not worry about what will eventually benefit us. After all, both of us are far removed from that question. But here is something that everyone could agree on. To listen to philosophers, it takes a great deal of practice in listening. Is this not true?

"What should I talk to you about, then? Tell me, what are you capable of hearing about? About what is good and evil? The good and evil of what? Maybe a horse?"

"No."

"Of an ox?"

"No."

"Of a human being?"

"Yes."

You must kindle the desire in a philosopher to talk to you

Do we know what a human being is? What his nature is? What the concept of a human being is? Do we have ears sufficiently open regarding this? Do you even have an idea of what nature is? Are you, to any extent, capable of following me as I speak?

Shall I demonstrate it for you? How can I? Do you understand at all what proof is, what demonstration is, and how a proof is demonstrated? What looks like proof, but is not? Can you tell the difference between what is true and what is false? Do you know what follows from what, what conflicts with what, what opposes what, and what is not in harmony with what?

What can I do to get you excited about philosophy? When you don't even know what contradiction is, how can I show you that most people have conflicting ideas about what is good and evil, and what is beneficial and harmful?

So, show me what I can accomplish by talking to you. Kindle a desire in me. When a sheep sees grass, it kindles a desire in the sheep to eat, but not if you offer it a stone or a loaf of bread. Similarly, some of us have a desire to speak if we come across a suitable listener who herself kindles such a desire. But if she sits like a stone, or grass, how can she kindle any such a desire? Does the vine say to the farmer "Look at me?" But it shows by the way it looks that anyone who cares for it will profit from it and so invites them to take care of it.

We get involved when our desire is kindled

Which of us turn down the invitation of charming little children to join in their games, crawl with them, and engage in baby talk? But who wants to play with a donkey and bray like it? Even if it is little, a donkey is a donkey.

"Why don't you say anything to me then?"

I have only this to say to you. Anyone who is ignorant of who they are, what they are born for, in what kind of world they find themselves in and whom they share it with; who does not know what things are good and bad, what are honorable and shameful; who is unable to follow argument or proof, and cannot tell the difference between what is true and what is false: such a person will exercise neither their desires, nor aversions, nor impulses, nor choices in accordance with nature. Being deaf and blind, they would go around thinking they are somebody, while they are nobody.

STOIC CHOICES • 153

Not knowing what is advantageous has created errors and misfortunes

Is there anything new in all this? Hasn't this been so since humanity began? Isn't this ignorance the cause of all our errors and misfortunes? Wasn't this why Agamemnon and Achilles fought each other? Wasn't it for not knowing what is to one's advantage and what is not? Did one of them say that it is advantageous to return Chryseis to her father, while the other said that it isn't? Did one of them say that it is advantageous to take away the other's prize, while the other said that it isn't? Did both not forget who they were and what they came for?

"What did you come for? To acquire a lover or to fight?"

"To fight."

"Against whom? The Trojans or the Greeks?"

"Against the Trojans."

"Will you then let Hector go and instead fight with your king? [And you, the king] desert your duties as a king, 'with nations to watch over and having so many cares.' You exchange blows with the greatest warrior among your allies when you should be treating him with respect and protecting him. And this over a girl. Are you inferior to the elegant high priest who treats noble warriors with every respect?"

Do you see the effect of not knowing what is advantageous?

"But I too am rich."

"What, richer than Agamemnon?"

"But I am handsome too."

"What, more handsome than Achilles?"

"But I have fine hair too."

"Wasn't Achilles' hair finer than yours? Wasn't it golden too? Didn't he comb it elegantly and dress it up?"

"But I am strong too."

"Can you then lift a stone of the size lifted by Hector or Aias?"

"But I am of noble family too."

"Is your mother a goddess or your father a god? Anyway, what good did it all do to Achilles when he sat crying for a girl?"

"But I am an orator too."

"Wasn't Achilles? Don't you see how he got the better of the most eloquent of the Greeks, Odysseus, and Phoenix? How he made them speechless? This is all I have to say to you. And even this, with reluctance."

"Why do you say that?"

"Because you haven't kindled my enthusiasm. What can I see in you that makes me comparable to a rider seeing a thoroughbred horse? Your poor body? You have treated it in a shameful way. Your clothes? Too luxurious. Your bearing and looks? Not worth a second glance."

When you want to hear a philosopher, don't say, "Have you nothing to say to me?" Instead, show that you can listen to the philosopher. You will then see then how you excite the speaker to talk to you.

Think about this

"Just as there is a skill in speaking, there is also a skill in listening." Discourses. II.24.5. Epictetus [RH]

Why is Logic Needed?

Key ideas of this discourse

1. *If you want to know why logic is important, one needs to develop a logical argument to show that.*
2. *But unless you know logic, you won't even know whether the argument is valid or misleading.*
3. *Therefore, logic is needed, even to decide if logic is needed.*

The proof for the need for logic

Someone asked Epictetus:

"Convince me that logic is useful."

"Would you like me to demonstrate it to you?"

"Yes."

"Then I must use a demonstrative argument."

"Agreed."

"How will you know if I am misleading you with a dishonest argument?"

"I don't know."

"Don't you see, you yourself are admitting that logic is necessary. Without it, you cannot even decide whether you need it or not."

Think about this

"Logic is necessary, since without it you can't even tell whether it is necessary or not." Discourses II.25.3. Epictetus [RH]

Become Skillful in Correcting Contradictions

Key ideas of this discourse

1. *People indulge in contradictory actions only because they don't know they are being contradictory and believe what they do is right.*
2. *If you point out their contradiction, they will change.*
3. *If they remain unconvinced, it means that you are not skilled enough to show them their contradiction.*

People who err do so because they are not aware of it

Every error involves a contradiction. Someone who commits an error doesn't want to do so but wants to act correctly. Clearly then he is not doing what he wants. What does a thief want to get? Something that would benefit him. If theft is not to his benefit, then he isn't doing what he wants. Now every rational mind is against contradiction. But if you don't realize that you are involved in a contradiction, there is nothing that stops you from being contradictory. When you come to realize it, you have no choice but give it up and avoid it. Out of bitter necessity, you are forced to give up what is false as soon as you realize it is false, even though you held on to it as true when you didn't know any better.

Someone skilled in argument, one who can support and disprove, will be able to show others their contradiction that causes them to err; and show that they are not doing what they want. If this is made clear to them, they would correct their error; but if you don't convince them, don't be surprised if they continue to do what they do because they believe it is right. This is the reason why Socrates said:

"I'm not in the habit of calling another witness to speak in support of what I am saying, but I always remain satisfied with the person who is engaging in discussion with me and call on his vote and summon him as witness, so that he alone suffices for me in the place of others." [Based on Xenophon's *Memorabilia*, III.9.8. Robin Hard's rendition.]

Socrates knew how to move a rational mind. It is like a balance and it will move, whether one likes it or not. Show our ruling rational faculty a contradiction, it will give it up. But if you fail to do so, blame yourself, not the person who remains unconvinced.

Think about this

Every rational mind is by nature averse to contradiction. But if someone fails to realize that he is involved in a contradiction, there is nothing to prevent him from carrying out contradictory actions. Discourses II.26.3. Epictetus [RH]

ABOUT THE AUTHOR

Dr Chuck Chakrapani has been a long-term, but embarrassingly inconsistent, practitioner of Stoicism. He is the president of Leger Analytics, Chief Knowledge Officer of The Blackstone Group in Chicago, and a Distinguished Visiting Professor at Ryerson University.

Chuck has authored books on several subjects over the years which include research methods, statistics, and investment strategies. His personal website is ChuckChakrapani.com

His books on Stoicism include *Unshakable Freedom*, *A Fortunate Storm* and *The Good Life Handbook* (a rendering of Epictetus' Enchiridion.)

ALSO BY THE AUTHOR

A Fortunate Storm

Three unconnected events – a shipwreck in Piraeus, a play in Thebes, and the banishment of a rebel in Turkey – connected three unrelated individuals to give birth to a philosophy. It was to endure 2,000 years.

Get a FREE COPY of the eBook at TheStoicGym.com

The Good Life Handbook

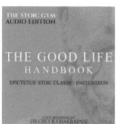

Available in print, digital, and audio editions, *The Good Life Handbook* is a rendering of *Enchiridion* in plain English.

Please get your copy in your favorite online bookstore.

Unshakable Freedom

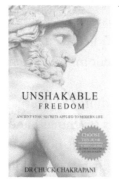

How can we achieve total personal freedom when we have so many obligations and so many demands on our time? Is personal freedom even possible?

Yes, it is possible, said the Stoics.

Stoicism in Plain English

Stoicism in Plain English books 1-5 represent the complete works of Epictetus.

Stoic Foundations (Discourses Book 1) explains the basic tenets of Stoicism.

Stoic Choices is the plain English version of Discourses Book 2. It revolves around themes of choice.

Stoic Training is the third book of *Discourses* of Epictetus in plain English. Stoics did not only believe in theoretical knowledge but held that it is critical we practice what we learned.

Stoic Freedom (Discourses Book 4) focuses on freedom. Personal freedom is close to Epictetus' heart, and his rhetoric shines when he talks about freedom. But, what does a free person look like?

Stoic Inspirations combines the Enchiridion (Epictetus' pupil Arrian's notebook summarizing his teachings) and the remaining fragments of the lost Discourses books. It completes the Stoicism in Plain English series on Epictetus from The Stoic Gym.

Stoic Lessons

Stoic Lessons is the complete works of Musonius Rufus (25-95CE), the man who taught Epictetus. While he was very well-known and respected during his time, he is less widely known now. He was a social activist, a proto-feminist, a vegetarian, and a minimalist.

The Complete Works of Marcus Aurelius

Meditations by Emperor Marcus Aurelius (121-180 CE) is probably the most beloved, uplifting, and widely read classic of Stoic philosophy.

Marcus ruled the greatest empire the world had seen up until his time. Yet he faced several problems, both personal and political.

Glimpse the private man behind the public persona.

Marcus Aurelius the Unknown completes The Stoic Gym's Plain English translation of the most popular stoic's complete works.

Get your copies in your favorite online bookstore.

Made in United States
Troutdale, OR
11/13/2023

14562668R00096